FASHION BLOGS

Concept & Idea by Kirstin Hanssen and Felicia Nitzsche

*d'*jongeHond

UITGEVERY
SINDS 2007

CONTENTS

FASHION BLOGS

FOREWORD by Kirstin Hanssen	6
NEWS & VIEWS	8
INTRODUCTION by Marieke Ordelmans	10
STYLE BUBBLE	12
LES MADS	19
DIANE, A SHADED VIEW ON FASHION	22
ISAAC LIKES	26
IGOR + ANDRÉ	30
THE COVETED	34
ABDUL LAGERFIELD	37
JULY STARS	42
SEEN ON THE STREETS	46
INTRODUCTION by Mrs. Mo Veld	48
GARANCE DORÉ	50
HEL LOOKS	54
STIL IN BERLIN	58
COPENHAGEN STREET STYLE	62
THE STREETS WALKER	66
THE STREETHEARTS	70
PERSONAL STYLE DIARIES	74
INTRODUCTION by Marten Mantel	76
SEA OF SHOES	78
ELINKAN	82
RENÉE STURME	85
MODERNITETER	88
PANDORA	92
CINDIDDY	96
NIOTILLFEM	99
LIEBE MARLENE VINTAGE	102
THE STYLISH WANDERER	106
GARBAGE DRESS	109
ALICE POINT	112
CREATURES OF THE NIGHT	116
INTRODUCTION by Aynouk Tan	118
GLAMCANYON	120
SHARK VS. BEAR	126
THE COBRA SNAKE	130
PRETEND IT NEVER HAPPENED	136
WHAT ABOUT THE BOYS?	140
INTRODUCTION by Carlo Wijnands	142
STYLE SALVAGE	144
KATELOVESME	148
STREET ETIQUETTE	152
THE DANDY PROJECT	155
MODE PARADE	158
BLOG INDEX	161

FOREWORD

The theme of this book first surfaced in 2005. People like Diane Pernet, Scott Schuman, and later also Susanna Lau took their first steps into the blogosphere: the kickoff to what would turn out to be one of the most highly acclaimed developments within fashion media. These web 2.0 pioneers have been an inspiration for thousands, and have generated an online revolution, celebrating its triumph in style.

The sweet blend of fashion blogs – everything from street style to young girls striking a pose in their latest greatest outfits, to the contemporary dandy chronicles and everything in between – inspired us to begin to develop this book in the summer of 2008. Felicia, Elina, and I knew that every single phrase in an internet-related book would be outdated by the time we finished it, and yet we felt the unstoppable urge to freeze-frame this magnificent phenomenon, and somehow encapsulate it into a fixed form - a printed record of zeitgeist if you will.

In the year that followed, we weren't surprised to see the popularity of some bloggers reach new heights, as we already knew that they would give the industry a breath of fresh air. It promoted fashion as a tool to express individuality, and as a means of advancing both upcoming and established brands and designers. And so the bloggers we initially perceived merely as talented teenagers, blogging from their tiny bedrooms in faraway villages, now made it to the front row and the backstage at fashion week. They were asked to judge at design graduation shows, they were featured in prominent media, they were given the opportunity to design their own fashion lines, and one even had a coveted designer bag named after him! Others took a different route and started a career in the fashion industry, working as editors, stylists, and photographers. The ultimate example of professional amateurism, and to what it can lead.

While making FASHION BLOGS and discussing each fashion blogger extensively amongst ourselves, we automatically started calling them by their first names, knowing all about where they resided, what they were doing from day to day, and (most importantly...) what they were wearing while doing it! This sense of familiarity is in all likelihood the key to the popularity of fashion blogs. Besides that, we were completely fascinated by the 'boundless exhibitionism' and 'shameless voyeurism' that seems to be part of some fashion blogs. The opportunity to intensively scrutinise the personal life of an utter stranger is something printed media aren't able to give. And why would they want to? After all, fashion magazines have their own unique strengths. With their huge budgets and unparalleled expertise, they can produce the type of content an individual blogger never could.

Fashion blogging has prompted a certain amount of discussion about the new vs. the traditional media. Or should we say: about the 'subjective' opinions of non-professional bloggers vs. the 'objective' perspectives of established editors? Some of our opinion leaders have even expressed concern about the internet granting power to isolated individuals, who can now blog or twitter criticism on brands or companies, which can then have a huge effect as others join in online. Fortunately, some industry insiders have indeed embraced fashion bloggers, as you can read in the five chapter introductions in this book.

by Kirstin Hanssen

So, what's next? We can only guess. Style blogs are most likely the established fashion media of tomorrow. In any case, we hope the fashion bloggers in this book will persevere, that their blogs will last, and that they retain the originality and authenticity we so admire and respect them for. And if for some reason they do not, they will still shine forever, like the ones in our inevitably incomplete, but carefully selected URL index.

Every era has its beginning. In this book you will find the result of what is happening now in the fashion blog world, a couple of years after the kick-off, but just a few hits before the big bang.

NEWS
& VIEWS

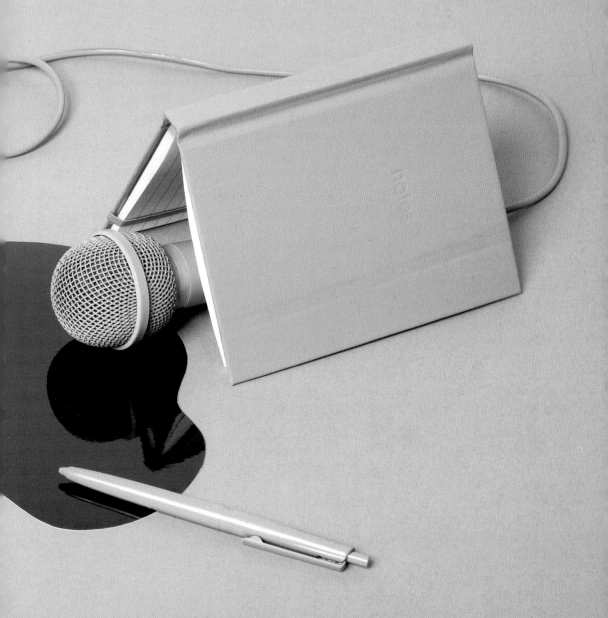

NEWS
& VIEWS

I'm backstage at London Fashion Week when my eye is drawn to an unusual figure. A mini-girl, in towering heels, short leather skirt, and colourful vintage top, is presenting her critical opinion on the clothes that were just shown. Her equally extravagantly dressed gay buddy, donning a striking full head of red curls, is taking photos. They are thirteen; fourteen at the most. I cannot keep my eyes off these kids. So young, and already so distinctive. So young, and already completely swallowed by the harsh fashion world. I think back to when I was thirteen, and suddenly find myself unsure whether to deem the scene before me fabulous, or in fact completely saddening. In any case, I do find them quite touching, these awfully young fashion icons, blogging as though their life depended on it.

Being a writer down to the bone, I myself also blog, expressing myself in words. Inspirations, irritations, fascinations; I pour everything in a textual form. I'm not an extraordinary and inspiring work of art that people want to stop and look at. I prefer to touch people with words. And yet we, the writers and personal style icons, have a lot in common. We share our passion for fashion with the world, through a blog. And together, we changed the fashion world from a closed universe into an open book of style, to which everyone can contribute.

With the arrival of the internet, the door to the fashion world was pushed ajar, and fashion bloggers subsequently kicked the door wide open. They are unhindered by borders or language barriers, and (in most cases) aren't reprimanded by editors and advertisers when they decide to turn left rather than right. They have their own opinion, style, and above all: they are extremely passionate and ambitious. Because without these character traits,

maintaining a blog would be impossible. Simple as it may seem to the outside world, filling a blog with content costs vast amounts of time and energy, and there isn't always a payback. This 'bedroom journalism' dominating the fashion world today is far greater than we think. Is the spotlight presently focused on a select group of bloggers, behind closed doors tens of thousands of fashion fantasts are blogging like there is no tomorrow. Day and night!

There is a group of a lucky few, which surprisingly consists mainly of style bloggers, that has started a chain reaction. By being an even greater source of inspiration than the Anna Wintour-dressed models in VOGUE, they have managed to turn fashion bloggers into a phenomenon, and we are all reaping the benefits. Traditional media are thrust from their front-row seats by fashion bloggers, designers use them as a soundboard, and marketing predators employ them to promote their products. With the immediacy of this personal medium, the large blogging community is now worth a fortune, and the fashion world is all too aware of it.

Admittedly, I don't visit style blogs often myself. Sure, I keep an eye on them. I find them fascinating, and in part, they are the thread of today's fashion trends. But I am not inspired by them personally. Their idiosyncratic style is too explicit for my taste. The well-known sense of 'me, myself and I' creeps up on me when I see photo shoot no. 1001. I rather prefer to be inspired by people on the street, spotted by heroes such as THE SARTORIALIST and Garance Doré. Unpolished, pure, unexpected. That, to me, is fashion.

by Marieke Ordelmans

ABOUT
Marieke Ordelmans

Marieke Ordelmans (1986) graduated from the Hogeschool van
Amsterdam (media & information
management) in 2008. For her
thesis, she studied the influence
of fashion blogs on the fashion
world, interviewing hotshots
such as Cathy Horyn (NEW YORK
TIMES), THE SARTORIALIST,
and Diane Pernet.
She began her career as a
fashion journalist working for
FASHION.BLOG.NL, and recently
founded the collaborative
THE DIGITALISTAS, a blog about
fashion, beauty, and lifestyle.
Marieke has published in noted
magazines and newspapers
such as ELLE, GRAZIA, CODE,
and DE VOLKSKRANT, and is currently writing her second novel.

www.thedigitalistas.com

FAVOURITE BLOGS
www.fashionista.com
+
www.garancedore.fr
+
www.fashionologie.com
+
www.runway.blogs.nytimes.com
+
www.fashionologie.com

STYLE BUBBLE

STYLE BUBBLE is the universe of Susanna Lau, a.k.a. Susie Bubble, one of the main inspirations for this book. In 2008 she was named among the EVENING STANDARD's '1000 most influential Londoners'. Having the status of fashion insider ("Oh I hate the word") and being recognised on the street are some of the side effects of fashion blogging the UCL history graduate is still not used to. "I don't think bloggers should think that it's their right to be famous."

STYLE BUBBLE: indefinable, not quite flawless, in a refreshing way. It's a one of a kind, colourful bouquet of professional views on fashion news, experimental dress-up sessions, jubilant discoveries of the odd, the avant-garde, and the talented, combined with personal notes. Besides that, STYLE BUBBLE is about shoes, as the British-born Chinese Miss Lau has a fetish for incredibly impractical high heels. But on the day we meet the down-to-earth Susanna Lau in Amsterdam, she is wearing simple black flats. For someone who travels the globe to report on various fashion weeks, she makes an amazingly relaxed impression. So, what's the story behind the name? "Susie Bubble isn't someone I invented, it's actually a nickname that I've had since I was ten. My best friend at primary school just started calling me that for some reason, because I was always daydreaming and drifting off to higher resorts. So that's where the bubble bit came from," Susanna explains. After graduating from UCL, she worked at a digital advertising company, later as an editor for DAZED DIGITAL. "I had no idea what I wanted to do when I came out of uni, and when I was still working at the advertising company I decided to start the blog. I always had a job alongside the blog to pay the bills."

Ancient

Although Susie is now often stopped in the street by STYLE BUBBLE fans, she still finds being recognised for blogging quite a strange thing. "You're just this person on the internet, typing things. You know roughly how many people are reading the blog, but you don't know exactly. People asking for autographs I think is a particularly strange one. In TOPSHOP, someone asked me to sign their bag, and I'm like: 'I ruined your tote, what are you going to do with that signature?' I was so disturbed by that, and I was bummed because I have a really lousy signature, it's like 'S Lau', it's not like it's 'Susie Bubble' or anything." Between all

BLOG TITLE
Style Bubble

URL
www.stylebubble.co.uk

EDITOR
Susanna Lau

YEAR OF BIRTH
1983

ONLINE SINCE
March 2006

COUNTRY
UK

LANGUAGE
English

POSTS PER WEEK
14-20

VISITORS PER DAY
20000

TAGS
cages, fashion week, high street, london, sheer, vintage

FAVOURITE BLOGS
www.ashadedviewonfashion.com
+
www.luxirare.com
+
www.kingdomofstyle.typepad.co.uk
+
www.the-coveted.com
+
www.pipeline.refinery29.com
+
www.jakandjil.com

by Kirstin Hanssen & Elina Tozzi

the media attention, being invited to fashion shows, and being recognised by absolute strangers, it may seem fashion blogging has become today's fast lane to fame, or to starting a career in the fashion industry. Susie disagrees: "Bloggers shouldn't think that it's their right to be famous, because it's really a transient thing that will pass in probably like a year or so. I've done this for three years, and I'm probably one of the older bloggers around. Yeah, I feel ancient! I don't really like this idea that there is now a group of up-and-coming bloggers that are blogging purely because they see it as their ticket into the fashion industry. I'm quite wary slash uncomfortable about giving advice on 'how to make your blog successful', because there is no straightforward recipe. I'll try to give my advice best I can, but I don't want to become some kind of blogging 'guru'. In fact, I was never one of those people that wanted to be an actual journalist, who wanted to study fashion. It sounds really bad, but I'm not sort of career-driven in general. I'm just not that super-ambitious person."

Freedom in blogging

As it usually happens when something is in vogue, there is a huge 'jumping on the bandwagon' going on around fashion blogs. With a blog as massively popular as STYLE BUBBLE, everybody must want a piece of its creator... "Yeah, I get two to three hundred emails a day, so going through emails is a job in itself. And you'll have the PR-companies approaching you about whatever blah blah blah stuff that's completely irrelevant to the blog, so I'll put that aside immediately. At the end of the day, if I don't like something, I'm simply not going to blog about it." However, there is also a positive side to being a prominent blogger, especially in relation to young designers. As Susie explains: "I do get designers who contact me about their work, to get featured on the blog, and I'm happy that they're approaching bloggers as well, because they recognise that it's a different platform and that their clothes aren't always going to be called in for magazines. I appreciate having the opportunity to view their collection."

A 'growing up thing'

Susanna began blogging on her personal STYLEHIVE page, the popular online fashion community. Comparing STYLE BUBBLE now to Susie's earlier blogging days, we notice her love for vintage has remained constant, though she does say: "I am a bit more selective with vintage. It's one of those things where you don't want to buy just any old thing. I actually do less shopping now than I did when I started the blog, just because I don't really have the time anymore. I used to just go into TOPSHOP and buy ten things, and I regret that, 'cause I don't wear those things anymore. So that's just a growing up thing. My money situation obviously changed as well, I'm a bit more prudent with my money now." About the advantages of rubbing elbows with designers, Susie can say: "It is true that I also get sent things, not from brands, more like independent designers, the people that I've talked about basically on the blog, and I've built relationships with them."

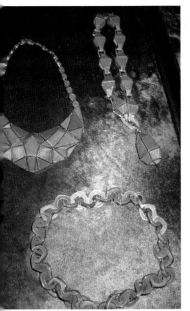

Style schizophrenia

Reading the endless comments of admiration on STYLE BUBBLE, one can imagine that Susie must be an inspiration for many girls. But Susie doesn't believe people emulate her style. "I have a very specific type of style. I'm not one thing or the other; in my style I'm very schizophrenic, like style schizophrenia, where I jump from one thing to the other. I'm quite experimental, but that's just the nature of my style anyway. I don't really mind if people take some facets of it, but what I really want to encourage through my blog is for people to find their own thing, which is why I don't just post about my personal style. 'Here's me, look at me', you know, 'aren't I so great?' It's not really about that."

Inner bitchiness

It's a fact known amongst insiders that personal style bloggers have to deal with more than just friendly feedback from readers. What conclusion has Susanna distilled from this? "People have inner bitchiness they want to express online. I personally have never felt the need to be anonymous and ghastly in that way, but the internet is such a dangerous place where you can do that. Obviously when I come across some blogs I think to myself 'oh god, what a loser', but I've never expressed it online. I suppose some people feel that they can cross that line and publish that negative comment because that it's so easy." Still, Susie thinks there may be more to this breaking of the 'netiquette' by commenters. Is it perhaps the true nature of girls that the medium brings out? "It's difficult to say. I think that some of the negative comments are also out of frustration, envy, or it might have touched a personal nerve."

Amazing editorials

So how is the success of the blogging phenomenon influencing printed media? "I think it just gets rid of the magazines that are not producing great content, that is not compelling to their readers, and it makes them push to excel at what they are good at, which is producing amazing editorials and doing seminal interviews with legendary figures", Susie answers. "With a lot of magazines the content is really throwaway. It's like 'top five tips to get a tan', 'top ten skirt shapes'. Okay, I didn't really need to pay two pounds to get that information! Blogs offer a different kind of information, though I don't think blogs produce the same kind of high-quality content that magazines do. It takes months and months of planning to do an interview, a shoot, or a feature. I don't know if you can necessarily try to replicate that, especially because with blogging, you're doing it on a day-to-day basis, and you're not really planning. They're just two completely different mediums and they should be complimentary, rather than competitive with each other. Classical media just need to be aware of what's going on on blogs, so that they can go back and use the information to do their own job better." And with this advice to the print media our interview with one of fashion blogging's most prominent voices ends. We look forward to seeing what Susie Bubble, beloved, respected, revered, will be doing next.

LES MADS

LES MADS are *les mademoiselles* **Julia Knoll and Jessica Weiss, the founders, who were joined in late 2008 by Jessica's younger sister Natalie Weiss. One of the first and now biggest fashion news blogs in Germany, LES MADS combines backstage fashion reports with personal views on the news, as well as the greatest latest outfits, reaching far beyond the German border. And what makes LES MADS even more worthwhile: their comprehensive collection of shopping guides, ranging from the best online vintage treasure chests to the finest boutiques in cities such as Stockholm, New York, and Berlin.**

German fashion blog scene

In contrast to Sweden and the USA, Germany still seems more of a slow developer in terms of fashion blogs. Jessie and Julia explain: "Since it's more flattering for a German woman to tell her she is smart than tell her she is beautiful, it is extra tricky to thrive in a superficial field like fashion. Besides this, there is a preference for criticism in Germany, and this threatens any lightness and the easy tones that creativity often requires."

News resources

The duo says they are particularly inspired by international magazines and events that happen in their nearby surroundings or on the street. "This is besides using GOOGLE READER, with feeds from 300 international blogs in different categories. We pick the stories and articles we like the most and rewrite them to make it the best possible article for our readers. Our holy bible is WWD.COM which keeps us well-informed alongside other press information or newsletters that we receive now."

Commercial network

LES MADS is now part of the commercial GLAM PUBLISHER network. "We weren't even aware that a concept like GLAM existed when we started the blog. But with the financial support from HUBERT BURDA MEDIA we were able to develop more specific ideas about growth and the various possibilities. We are very happy that GLAM selected us to be one of the sites to join the network when they planned to enter the German market. It caused us to change our blog layout, because it now integrates advertisements."

BLOG TITLE
Les Mads

URL
www.lesmads.de

EDITORS
Jessica Weiss, Julia Knolle, Natalie Weiss

YEAR OF BIRTH
1986, 1982, 1988

ONLINE SINCE
April 2007

COUNTRY
Germany

LANGUAGE
German

POSTS PER WEEK
35

VISITORS PER DAY
7000

TAGS
lifestyle, outfits

FAVOURITE BLOGS
www.ytligheter.com
+
www.lealoves.blogspot.com
+
www.lalila.de
+
www.garbagedress.com

by Kirstin Hanssen

Recognition for online writers

"As with any other evolving hype, there is always a moment when hobbies turn into obsessions," Jessica remarks on the developments in fashion blogging. "Despite the rising number of new blogs, we are very happy about the rather late, but nonetheless increasing external recognition online writers are receiving through industry-related brands and companies. Besides that, print journalism had to move a tiny little step to the side when it comes to coverage of time-sensitive events such as unveiling collections during fashion week. For the future, we hope fashion blogs will grow and get better every day, to live happily ever after in a peaceful co-existence with print media. Above all, to have an audience thankful for innovative ways of delivering information."

DIANE, A SHADED VIEW ON FASHION

Diane Pernet is a true fashion icon and the world is her playground. Her striking appearance cannot be missed at the numerous events she reports on for her blog A SHADED VIEW ON FASHION: one of the three most influential fashion blogs, according to the MOMA (New York). "It is a filter for what I like in fashion, art, music, architecture, and design. The idea of the blog is to shine a light on creativity around the planet," the veiled lady comments.

Pernet, a Paris-based journalist, has a long career in the fashion circuit. She was designer of her own cult-brand, before moving on to journalism. After working at ELLE.COM and VOGUEPARIS.COM, she decided she wanted to create a platform that was unconstrained by advertisers, and thus started her legendary blog. Pernet explains: "I like the immediacy of a blog as opposed to an internet site or the time lag that is necessary for a print publication. That said, I am the co-editor in chief for ZOO MAGAZINE and also write for other print publications." A SHADED VIEW is therefore not Diane's main activity, though she admits this could change if blogging were to become more profitable/gainful, financially. "My primary interest is building my film festival A SHADED VIEW ON FASHION FILM (ASVOFF) and finding new sponsors for that and for my blog." Here, Pernet momentarily lifts the veil on her busy fashion-filled life.

What are your news resources?
"I have a great personal network. That, combined with my travels, is my best resource. Further, I enjoy BUSINESS OF FASHION: the way they highlight the most interesting fashion articles saves me time, it's very efficient. I also like the JC REPORT."

You stated that one of your visions is to make fashion democratic. What does this mean exactly and how do you contribute to this cause?
"Making fashion democratic means offering it to everyone, all over the planet. That is what I do and so I think that vision is a reality. How do I contribute to the cause? I travel a lot and I am a talent scout. When I find interesting people, I put a post about them on my blog. They then get agents, shops, and press. It works very well for them, because the industry uses my site as a resource."

BLOG TITLE
Diane, a Shaded View On Fashion

URL
www.ashadedviewonfashion.com

EDITOR
Diane Pernet

YEAR OF BIRTH
-

NATIONALITY
American

CATEGORY
Fashion Journalism

ONLINE SINCE
February 2005

COUNTRY
France

LANGUAGE
English

POSTS PER DAY
8

VISITORS PER DAY
5000-6000

TAGS
creation, fashion, global

FAVOURITE BLOGS
www.businessoffashion.net
+
www.nicolaformichetti.blogspot.com
+
www.showstudio.com
+
www.dazeddigital.com
+
www.stylebubble.co.uk

by Kirstin Hanssen

photos: (clockwise from top left) KIDS at the Palace in Seoul, with Jean-Charles de Castelbajac at his home, Susie Bubble with Hannah Marshall at London Fashion Week, with Henrik Vibskov in Seoul, with Diesel's Renzo Rosso at ITS 7 Trieste, with Steve J & Yoni P in Seoul

How important are stats for you and for your motivation to keep going?

"Like anyone, you feel great when they zoom up, and not great when they dip down. Nonetheless, it is the quality of the viewers that is of value to advertisers, more so than the quantity."

Why did you decide to work with other contributors and how do you select them?

"My site is about the planet, not just Paris, and even if I travel a lot, there is a lot of territory to cover and one person cannot do it all. For example, Sonny Vandevelde has a blog and he also does the best backstage photos for my site. When I travel, I meet people, and if I think they have a good insider's view of their city and I enjoy reading them, I ask them to contribute. Sometimes people also come up to me and ask if they can contribute."

What is the most remarkable thing that has happened since you started blogging?

"The most fun was when Mark Eley of ELEY KISHIMOTO asked me to do a road movie on his menswear launch. It involved being in the support car for the GUMBALL 3000. We covered 3000 miles in six days and, along with filming it, I lifeblogged the entire way. Another time, I received an offer to curate a fashion and photography exhibition in Santiago de Compostela from Shaded Viewers."

What can you say about the development of fashion blogs over the past years?

"Well, when I started there really weren't any, or maybe only very few fashion blogs. There were political blogs, so I was a bit of a pioneer. Now, there are thousands of fashion blogs, which I think is great. Bloggers are being taken more seriously. In the case of someone like Susie Bubble, it turned into a fashion job at DAZED DIGITAL, and for THE SARTORIALIST it turned into quite a money-making experience. I am all for developing internet television, and I like original points of view."

Do you think the growing influence of blogging is altering the role of fashion magazines?

"The fact that all print publications now have blogs and that their blogs often contain videos already shows the influence of the internet. A lot of people collect most of their information from the web now, rather than from magazines and newspapers. Businesses do their market research through blogs. The thing with a blog is the information stays on the internet forever, but it travels quickly down the page. Magazine articles are usually longer and you can read them also when you don't feel like being behind the computer. Nevertheless, I think as soon as advertisers realise the reach of the internet as compared to the print magazines, they will place more of their budgets on the internet, and less on print."

ISAAC LIKES

Isaac Hindin Miller loves a good story. Noticing that journalists always have the best seats at fashion shows, this New Zealander decided the key to getting ahead is indeed getting started. Now, Isaac travels the world, rubbing elbows with designers, models, editors and photographers for his blog ISAAC LIKES, and trying to get the inside scoop on all that is fashion.

But don't expect to find Isaac dishing any dirt: as a follower of the Baha'i faith, he refrains from gossip and chooses instead to focus on the facts. Providing a personal account and insider anecdotes is his main objective, ultimately on every major cultural event worldwide. For now, however, he opts to focus on fashion exclusively, and doing a pretty solid job at getting the backstage stories. And what helps: he doesn't always have to sneak into fashion shows anymore like he did before: he actually gets *invited*.

Why did you start ISAAC LIKES?
"I've always loved writing, I've always loved sharing my thoughts and I've always been obsessed with fashion, so starting a blog seemed like a sensible decision. I was fed up with what I saw as a lack of real critique in the New Zealand fashion media, so I wanted to get in on the action and shake things up a bit."

What is the most remarkable thing that has happened since you started blogging?
"I've managed to travel to Paris, Milan, Berlin, Sydney and New York all in one year, so I guess I'm living my dream, and that's pretty cool! I love the travel, I love the feeling of success when you achieve something - even if it's just sneaking into a show - and I love all the crazy things I see and people I meet along the way. Sneaking backstage at CHANEL COUTURE and standing about a metre away from Karl Lagerfeld while the show was going on was pretty remarkable I think."

Do you have any tips for sneaking into a fashion show?
"Coming from New Zealand is not ideal when you're travelling to international fashion weeks - most of the designers don't even stock their clothes there. So there's no way I could get into PRADA or DIOR without sneaking in - so far I've had no luck with either though. My best tip is to

BLOG TITLE
Isaac Likes

URL
www.isaaclikes.com

EDITOR
Isaac Hindin Miller

YEAR OF BIRTH
1984

ONLINE SINCE
March 2008

COUNTRY
New Zealand

LANGUAGE
English

POSTS PER WEEK
21

VISITORS PER DAY
2500

TAGS
anecdotes, encounters, opinions

FAVOURITE BLOGS
www.thefashionisto.com
+
www.purple-diary.com
+
www.rag-pony.blogspot.com

by Elina Tozzi

be a 100% detached, always walk confidently and purposefully, and never allow a security guard to ask you where your invitation is. As soon as you get stuck in a conversation, it's all over. I've been caught plenty of times - I always get caught when it's a show I care a lot about. Security guards seem to have a sixth sense for desperation."

How does the fact that you are writing from New Zealand influence your blog?

"New Zealand is a tiny country and we're very proud of our own. So it's one of those situations where if a New Zealander becomes successful, we all claim it. The most New Zealand thing about my blog is how I spend so much time talking about what New Zealand models are doing overseas, every little success and triumph. So in that sense I guess ISAAC LIKES is a very patriotic Kiwi blog!"

How does your being a Baha'i follower influence your work as a fashion blogger?

"The Baha'i faith is all about creating unity and eliminating prejudices so I try not to write nasty things about people or to encourage gossip. I'll write critically about a company but never about a person. It's difficult sometimes - especially when it comes to anonymous commenters - but it is something I'm always trying to do. Also, I try to put a positive spin on everything. It is ISAAC *LIKES* after all!"

How do you deal with negative or bitchy comments?

"Negative comments used to bother me a lot more than they do now, but I've gotten so used to them that now I just take them in my stride. There are a lot of anonymous comments that are simply ridiculous, but every now and again somebody says something that smacks you straight in the face with a truthful statement. If people are commenting negatively, you sometimes need to take it as constructive criticism. I can't stand it when people say hateful things about other people though. That's the worst."

Why exactly did you state that you like fashion, but dislike the fashion industry?

"I love the fashion industry but I guess I see a lot of problems with it - the exploitation of young models and the superficiality of it all, but I don't think I can complain too loudly because I'm not doing much to put an end to any of it. Sometimes I get disillusioned with the industry and with how I respond to it, because it's so easy to get sucked in to. I think everything always seems much more glamorous from the outside. When I write truthfully about my bad experiences, like I did when I was in Berlin earlier this year, people often respond very negatively and feel like I take it all for granted. But I think it's better to be honest than to heap praise on people or events just because they're conceived as being cool."

What is the biggest regret you ever had in terms of blogging?

"There have been times when I've regretted not being more honest or standing my ground on an important issue, but I don't have too many regrets. You have to learn from all of your mistakes - I make a lot - but hopefully I'm getting better as I go??"

What kind of reader do you envision when you are writing your blog?
"I like to think that I write about fashion in a way that makes it accessible for people who aren't insane followers of the industry. So I guess everybody from my mum and my non-fashion loving friends to the most crazed fans dying for the latest news about models."

"What in fashion blogging do you think is overrated?
I'm not sure what's overrated, but I'll tell you what's underrated: writing. There are so many amazing blogs out there that get let down by shoddy spelling and grammar. Bloggers need to proofread their work!"

The secret behind my success is...
"Persistence and stickability!"

IGOR
+ ANDRÉ

Danny Roberts is the young Californian artist behind the blog IGOR + ANDRÉ. This photographer/fashion designer-come-illustrator has become famous for his artwork of all things fashion, notably his portraits of fellow fashion bloggers. He began drawing the portraits in 2008 as a sort of ode to all the beautiful and stylish blogging girls and guys that inspired him. The 'blogger portrait series' exhibit Roberts' unique style: cartoonesque, dreamlike, and somewhat eerie. These, and Danny's other illustrations now appear everywhere, from fashion blogs to magazines and even on garments. Danny tells us exactly how this love-affair with fashion blogs got started, and we try to get him to spill the beans on his blog's curious title...

Why did you decide to start IGOR + ANDRÉ?
"I'm a fashion artist living in Southern California. It's kind of funny how it came about... I was always intimidated by blogs, and I didn't know much about them. Back in April of 2008, my brother was doing internet research for the company he works for, and he ended up talking me into doing a blog so that he could practice things he learned at work. Then I started having fun with it and: *voilà*, the rest is history. It's really been fun blogging."

How did you get started as an illustrator?
"In kindergarten, school was half-day. My dad was the principal and mom the assistant principal of the high school connected to my school. So, when school was over, I would take paper out of my mom's office and draw comic books to sell to the high-schoolers during their lunch. To my mom's surprise, I sold all of them. We found out later the reason the comics were selling was the paper I drew on had students' phone numbers on the other side, so boys were buying my comics to get girls' numbers. I didn't mind."

What does the name IGOR + ANDRÉ stand for?
"Actually, I haven't really said why it's called that yet. It's named after a project I've been planning for the last two years, but it's not ready yet. Sorry about that."

BLOG TITLE
Igor + André

URL
www.igorandandre.blogspot.com

EDITOR
Danny Roberts

YEAR OF BIRTH
1985

ONLINE SINCE
April 2008

COUNTRY
USA

LANGUAGE
English

POSTS PER WEEK
3-5

VISITORS PER DAY
1800

TAGS
art, inspiration

FAVOURITE BLOGS
www.leblogdebetty.com
+
www.misspandora.fr
+
www.knighttcat.blogspot.com
+
www.fashiontoast.com
+
www.tavi-thenewgirlintown.
blogspot.com

by Elina Tozzi

How much time do you spend on blogging and on reading other fashion blogs?

"I spend 3-4 hours a day blogging, researching blogs, or commenting and reading blogs. I read tons of blogs. I follow LE BLOG DE BETTY, PANDORA, KNIGHT CAT, FASHION TOAST, Tavi. I would say they are helping shape the media world. I think they influence up-and-coming style trends. Also, I think they give an everyday voice and opinion on fashion that resonates with people across the world."

What is the most remarkable thing that has happened since you started blogging?

"I think it's been working with and designing a little collection for Gwen Stefani's HARAJUKU LOVERS."

What made you decide to start portraying fashion bloggers?

"A blogger from Sweden named Arvida Byström featured my art on her site, which was the first time that had happened, so I decided to paint a picture of her as a thank you. From that point on, I did portraits of bloggers that inspired me."

What was the most memorable reaction you received on a portrait?

"I had done a portrait of Louise Ebel of the blog PANDORA, and the next day I woke to read one of the most beautiful reviews of my art I had ever read."

Why do you think you are so attracted to fashion?

"I'm not sure why, but there is something about fashion that really inspires me. Fashion is kind of a door into a dream world for me, and I like entering that dream world."

What do you hope to achieve with IGOR + ANDRÉ?

"To reach and inspire as many people as I can, to make art."

THE COVETED

Jennine Tamm Jacob is quite the entrepreneur. While writing her successful blog, THE COVETED, Tamm Jacob decided fashion bloggers needed a place to gather advice on how to make their hard work count - financially that is. She founded INDEPENDENTFASHIONBLOGGERS.ORG in September of 2007, which has become known and supported by fashion enthusiasts worldwide ever since.

In doing so, Jennine tapped into the massive upswing of online advertising, and has become somewhat of an authority in the field, meanwhile still figuring out how to earn some sort of a living with her own blog. As Tamm Jacob explains: "The monetization process hasn't been easy. I'm earning more than I was when I just started, though making what I made before I started blogging... well that's a ways off." THE COVETED features the latest on style and fashion, with a focus on emerging designers, eco-friendly apparel, and beauty, but it is Jennine's voice and personal perspective that make the blog so captivating.

How did your blog get started?
"THE COVETED was born out of my own obsessive behaviours, shopping, reading fashion blogs, scrolling through EBAY for hours on end. When I started it, I think I was just obsessed with clothes, but as time went on, it became apparent that clothes have a lot of interesting aspects beyond 'cute' and 'on sale'. My blog is really a documentation of the process of finding all these interesting things about the ritual each of us performs every day: getting dressed."

How do you think the world of fashion blogs has changed in the past years?
"In the past few years, the quality of blogs has really gone up. I'm not saying that blogs were crap in the past, but there are more outstanding bloggers who really take their time and craft wonderful posts now. It used to be okay to use a crappy digicam and take an out of focus picture of your outfit in a mirror, but now you see really gorgeous photography on blogs. In that sense, people have become way more creative, not just with their clothes, but with their presentation."

BLOG TITLE
The Coveted

URL
www.the-coveted.com

EDITOR
Jennine Tamm Jacob

YEAR OF BIRTH
1975

ONLINE SINCE
February 2007

COUNTRY
USA

LANGUAGE
English

POSTS PER WEEK
7

VISITORS PER DAY
1500-2000

TAGS
beauty, personal style, vintage

FAVOURITE BLOGS
www.stylebubble.co.uk
+
www.imelda.com.au
+
www.liebemarlene.blogspot.com

by Elina Tozzi

Do you think the growing influence of blogging is altering the role of fashion magazines?

"Absolutely. The web format is more nimble than print, it can adapt much faster. That said, with the current issues around fashion, retailers going bankrupt, and designers pulling out of fashion week, magazines are going to have to find a way to develop a relationship with their readers beside the current situation of 'latest' and 'exclusive'. The nature of blogging has always been a conversation, and with all the chaos going on in the fashion industry, bloggers have not slowed down the conversation, or run out of things to say."

How do you see the future of your blog and of fashion blogs in general?

"When I started THE COVETED it was just me, now there is one other writer, Sonja Shin Hodgkins for Beauty. Having someone else working with me on the blog is really great, not just because it forces me to think about the content and how to balance it out for the readers. Since blogs seem to be growing in power, I think it's only natural that blogs become more professional, requiring more people to work on them. It's impossible to do everything alone."

ABDUL LAGERFIELD

The two most photographed and talked-about Dutchmen within the fashion blogosphere are, without question, stylist Sonny Groo, a.k.a. ABDUL LAGERFIELD, and his famous friend, colleague, and partner in crime Jean-Paul Paula. Ever since a photo titled 'Watchmen' appeared of Sonny and his 'posse', taken by JAK & JIL photographer Tommy Ton, his visual omnipresence within the international fashion in-crowd has increased tremendously. Still, the MYKROMAG founder says, praise and attention in the digital world do not necessarily guarantee actual (offline) success.

It is a lazy, sunny afternoon when Sonny arrives on his bicycle at the location of our interview. As usual, he is clad head to toe in immaculate black, but this isn't the only thing that makes him stand out on the streets of Amsterdam. Whether it is his perfect straight hairdo or his big black diamond-adorned LANVIN sunglasses, somehow we just cannot take our eyes off Sonny... When asked about his equally remarkable name, he explains that he began inventing nicknames for friends as a teenager, simply for fun. "I started to call different people names that had no direct relation to their look or to them as an actual person. A typical blond preppy Dutch girl would get a name like Laquisha, or a big guy with a 'ghetto look' would be named Kees. Then I got into adding kind of 'fashion' surnames to them, and that's how I acquired the name Abdul Lagerfield." He quickly discovered how to use his online name and persona to his advantage. "At a certain point, all the major magazines' fashion editors, artists, photographers, and writers joined MYSPACE as well. All the people you so desperately wanted to work with and come into contact with. Having an appealing profile page enabled that." The black-haired Dutch boy with the big dreams managed to make a name for himself, one that he seems permanently stuck with. "Now, I wouldn't mind getting rid of the name Abdul Lagerfield, but it has worked so well for me that I will continue to use it for now. My real last name is a typically Dutch surname longer than Groo, but I am not going to reveal what that is!"

The making of a fashion blog icon

So how did Sonny Groo become who he is today, high heels and all? From an early age, the autodidact experimented with his appearance. "I received a liberal upbringing, I was able to wear and say what

BLOG TITLE
Abdul Lagerfield

URL
www.abdul-lagerfield.blogspot.com

EDITOR
Sonny Groo

YEAR OF BIRTH
1987

ONLINE SINCE
June 2007

COUNTRY
The Netherlands

LANGUAGE
English

POSTS
-

VISITORS
-

TAGS
backstage, designers, models

FAVOURITE BLOGS
www.bryanboy.com
+
www.jakandjil.com
+
www.coutequecoute.blogspot.com
+
www.theimagist.com
+
www.thefashionisto.com

by Elina Tozzi & Kirstin Hanssen

I wanted to. When I was a teenager I had blue hair for a while." Since then, Sonny has grown up quite a bit, gaining insight into the importance of appearance and image "Now, I am very conscious of what I wear, what I say, and do. I realise that image is crucial, and it's even becoming more important. My blog attributes to this idea. When I just started ABDUL LAGERFIELD, I wrote a lot of personal stories, whereas now, I choose to leave out my personal life." Sonny interned at a PR-agency in Amsterdam, attending a private styling course on the side. Styling jobs started to roll in, and Sonny was nominated for an ELLE STYLE AWARD in the category Stylist of the Year. In 2009, Sonny initiated an online magazine and platform for creative talent, MYKROMAG, a name derived from the word micro-organism. "You could say I'm self-made. It's a matter of love and passion, combined with practical experience, that enables you to grow. I always wanted to get into styling: to work for a magazine, in fashion. Of course, the reality of it is different. How do you manage to get where you want to be, how can you earn a living for yourself, how fake is the industry, how much fun is it? Now that I'm working on MYKROMAG, I'm also starting to find out that I enjoy bringing people together, to bring something to the next level together."

Perseverance is the key to success
Now that Sonny has appeared on countless blogs and been interviewed by magazines, we can ask him: does publicity determine success?
"It doesn't make a huge difference," he answers. "You can see your face splattered everywhere, but in the end, you do actually need to do the work that earns you a living. But publicity does help me in some ways. For instance, I don't require an introduction at model or press agencies. Jean-Paul and I have been visiting the fashion weeks for the past seven seasons. But there was a time when Jean-Paul and I were denied access. We were laughed at and people thought 'Who the hell are these hysterical dudes?' So in the end it all comes down to persevering, but also to achieving something real. It certainly wasn't just handed to me." Although Sonny agrees that his career would have progressed much more slowly if he had grown in an internet-less time, he says that: "You have to be either very bold or extremely good at what you do. Either way, you still need to stand out somehow. You need to be innovative."

Pushing boundaries
There are many things that could be said about Sonny and his friends, but not being innovative and different isn't one of them. "I try, along with Jean-Paul, to push boundaries, without actually crossing them. We wear heels and women's clothing. We represent a few trademarks such as unisex, androgyny, the mixing of cultures, and affordable clothes. People identify with that. For instance, about eighty percent of what I wear is from H&M. I think H&M is genius. And when I posted this opinion, I received an incredible amount of responses from people saying they were so happy I wrote that, because they too were living on a budget, buying their clothes at H&M." But with the pushing of boundaries comes controversy, and it isn't all praise and adoration that Sonny receives. As he explains: "There are plenty of haters around. In general I handle that kind

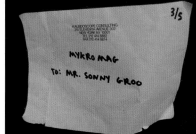

photos by Marco van Rijt, Duy Quoc Vo (portrait Jean-Paul Paula)

of thing really well, except when that 'Watchmen' photo appeared and we received such an incredible amount of hateful comments. I was kind of taken aback by that. People said we are over-styled, over-conceptualised, or that we always look the same. It just comes down to people wanting to vent their opinion, and not understanding, or not wanting to. I think that here in The Netherlands people are especially sober. In New York I could dress like a SESAME STREET character and no one would look twice."

The window as computer screen

Ideas about the future is something Sonny's brain seems to be overflowing with. For instance, he believes that everyone will wear sleek, dark materials in the future, and that the focus that now lies on appearance and image will shift to personalities. But he also doesn't shy away from more specific and detailed predictions, as he foresees that because every magazine and company will soon have its own blog, the necessity to stand out and take the next step will be created. "So then you'll connect a magazine to an exhibition, a book, a limited edition, or a movie," he says. "Multimedia is the future. Philips is going to produce a touch-screen window. That would mean magazines would be able to have their newest issue featured on the street; on a touch-screen!" This isn't just a pipe dream, as Sonny is already making similar plans for his own magazine. "This is the intention for MYKROMAG, whether in cooperation with commercial brands or not, as long as it is innovative and unexpected." So, we wonder, will Sonny be able to stay his unique self and also to stand his ground when associating with big commercial companies? He says: "When I do business, I do it well, and I don't take the easy route. I just say: if you're willing to invest some money, let's go ahead and have some fun with it. Let's flip it! If I can do that, and have financial independence, as well as stimulate and excite people, I'll be happy. After all, together *is* the future."

JULY STARS

Two stars were born in July. This is the sweet little story behind JULY STARS, the fashion blog of British/French Jaja Hargreaves. The title refers to both Jaja and her husband's month of birth and to the starry night skies of Southern France. For the London-based writing talent Jaja it seems that the sky is not the limit.

Jaja Hargreaves, who works as a professional translator, has a knack for combining her observations on fashion with photo collages. "Fashion is in my cultural background. My grandmother was a seamstress and growing up, I found myself transfixed by my mother's style: a combination of French chic and lots of exquisite bohemian antique jewellery. As a child, you'd invariably find me hidden in my parent's library, reading art and photography books or cutting pages out of my mum's fashion magazines. Writing about style is what drives me, carefully detailed fashion depictions and narratives, without being drily academic."

Why did you start JULY STARS?
"I started my blog in March 2008 for a variety of reasons: prominent among them was the desire to connect with people who share my views and fashion vision, to justify my opinions on style in writing, and to see if I could hold the reader's attention effectively. My key themes are always fashion designers, fashion stories, or fashion photography, with the occasional reference to my own experience or a comic element. The blog is a platform I use to close the gap between writing and fashion. I'm hoping to find my own convincing prose style and individual voice while focusing on subjects I love. In my notes, I only cover people or topics I'm interested in, and carefully select what I like from an inexhaustible fashion repertoire. I think it is important to stay honest and loyal to my individual taste, rather than wrestle with perhaps more popular ideas in a hugely competitive blogosphere."

What is the most remarkable thing that has happened since you started blogging?
"I've met wonderful people, people who identify with the blog and respond extremely positively to my writing. I've been invited to shows and asked to write for several fashion publications. I was also a finalist in the DAZED & CONFUSED fashion digital award competition."

BLOG TITLE
July Stars

URL
www.july-stars.com

EDITOR
Jaja Hargreaves

YEAR OF BIRTH
1976

ONLINE SINCE
March 2008

COUNTRY
UK

LANGUAGE
English

POSTS PER WEEK
2-3

VISITORS PER DAY
-

TAGS
fashion photography, writing

FAVOURITE BLOGS
www.garancedore.fr
+
www.decadediary.typepad.com
+
www.turnedout.tv
+
www.thisisnaive.com
+
www.fashiongonerogue.com

by Kirstin Hanssen

What are your news resources?

"I read a disconcertingly enormous amount of fashion blogs and magazines. Anything from French VOGUE, JALOUSE, PURPLE, SELF SERVICE,
LULA, RUSSH, ENCENS, FANTASTIC MAN, MONOCLE, POP, and NYLON,
to the more conventional fashion publications like ELLE, UK VOGUE,
GRAZIA, and the style supplement of the FINANCIAL TIMES. I sometimes
visit the Japan Centre in London to buy obscure Japanese magazines.
My fascination is insatiable!"

**The average age of fashion bloggers is astoundingly low; do you have
any idea as to why this is?**

"The majority of fashion blogs created by young people tend to move
in the same direction and focus on the same subjects. The competition
is formidable and few stand out. Style blogs are incredibly popular and
growing in numbers, but I can only think of four or five that are charming,
modest, and original. Blogs can have an immense magnetism and have
been triumphant in recent years, attracting and encouraging a lot of
young or very young people to start their own. In many ways, these tend
to be quite weak, copying each other, and are essentially vacuous."

**One of your posts is called 'We are all exhibitionists'.
Can you tell us a bit more about this?**

"I think that the internet has opened the doors to so much fashion
information and image, at the same time promoting a sort of culture
of personality, with a lot of fashion kids promoting so-called style blogs
to the detriment of quality and authenticity. That is just one of the
notorious scenarios that has unfolded alongside the natural flow of
technology evolution."

What would be your ultimate dream come true in terms of blogging?
"To write for a magazine I admire and respect!"

**How do you think the world of fashion blogs has changed in the
past years, and what do you think the future holds for fashion blogs?**
"People are increasingly turning to the internet to get their fashion
information, allowing fashion blogs to become legitimate and important
vehicles for news or inspiration. The fact that BURBERRY, VUITTON,
and MCQUEEN made the decision to show their spring/summer 2010
collection simultaneously on a catwalk and a live stream clearly marked
a new step in the world of fashion. It's a symbolic statement. The internet
plays the role of increasing equality. Fashion blogs will continue to be
enjoyed by increasing numbers of readers and internet users, but those
with visionary quality, variety of approach, and persuasive content will
be the most frequented."

**Do you think the growing influence of blogging is altering the role
of fashion magazines?**
"I don't believe that printed magazines will be phased out, but it is
very hard now to imagine an environment in which the internet is not
a destination in itself. I still love magazines, turning the pages, looking
through series of images. It's a more intense experience with a more
lasting and profound impact. When I look at fashion photography in
particular, I genuinely believe that compositions, colours, effects, and
patterns are more vibrant on print. I'm not saying that these qualities
are necessarily compromised on the web, but there is a certain flatness
you would never get with a magazine."

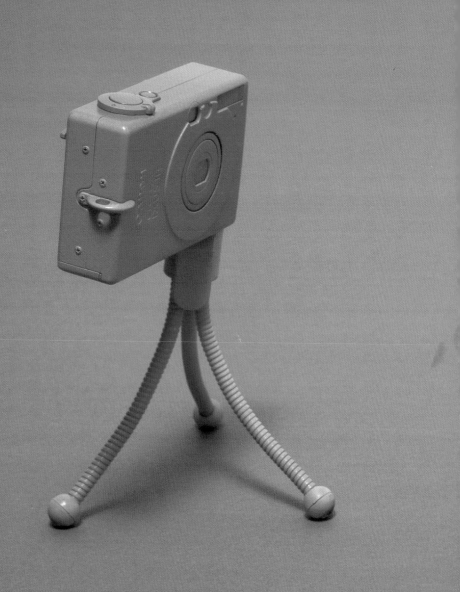

SEEN ON THE STREETS

SEEN ON THE STREETS

In order to explain my ecstatic praise for the web 2.0, with its mind-blowing 'blogosphere', and more specifically those blogs sharing everyday fashion reality ('street style'), I must, as I often seem to do these days, hark back to my humble beginnings in fashion and media. Being fourty (with a tiny little plus) means my professional heydays coincided with the rather premature birth of the internet, which was phenomenal for a handful of geeks, but pretty useless for fashion editors like myself at the time. It's the early nineties and I am the rookie fashion editor of an independent pop culture magazine (called BLVD.) in Amsterdam. Next to the highly experimental and conceptual fashion shoots with budding talents now known as Dutch fashion and photography royalty, we zoomed in on the street a lot. Firstly because that is where we knew our people, and people knew people, in real time and offline. Whatever the subject, music, art, technology or fashion - the latter was somehow always part of the story - we were looking for something authentic, alternative, daring, positive. Without realising it, we were cultural hackers, quite like bloggers today, and looking back now I think the nineties had a 'power-to-the-people-future' written all over it.

In one particularly successful and long-running series we picked hipsters of different walks of life and scenes from the street and literally dissected their outfits down to the details, deciphering their codes, origins, associations, and insider secrets. The 'models' became storytellers, and we filled in the gaps they typically mistook for common knowledge. I also remember how the popularity of this monthly feature, with readers and advertisers alike, took the publisher's sales department completely by surprise. The concept was extremely simple and it hit a note that would build up to be one of the

strongest cultural baselines in the decades to follow. Magazines such as i-D and THE FACE, or BLVD. on a more local level, were fiercely progressive in showing that high and low culture, mainstream and underground, the establishment as much as the individual, were at the very least equally directional forces. In pace with new technologies, the general attitude became more and more DIY. Remix professionals like DJ's and fashion stylists stepped up to the centre stage, and new professions like 'cool hunter' emerged. Now the new job titles are 'blogger' or even 'twitterer'. New times bring new dynamics bring new jobs. Nothing new there.

Around the turn of the century (I love how that sounds really old), I made my first trip to Japan. The country and its culture had fascinated me for a long time and for many reasons, but even though Japanese fashion designers like Rei Kawakubo and Yohji Yamamoto were already immortal gods at the time, I hadn't really considered Japan a fashion nation. Until I started walking the streets of Tokyo and Osaka. Never had I seen so many well-dressed tweens, displaying an unusually informed sense of style and unbridled fashion enthusiasm. There were excesses like the Cosplay scene, spending their weekends on the curb being photographed while dressing each other up in the most phantasmagorical costumes. Much more impressive to me was the omnipresent, totally everyday and seemingly effortless-looking celebration of fashion and personal style. These too were being photographed in the streets all the time. Japanese magazines employed tons of street fashion photographers and soon these highly *kawaii* Japanese street fashion shots started popping up in European magazines. I guess somehow, somewhere, this typical Japanese

by Mrs. Mo Veld

enthusiasm for fashion and styling, completely weary of cynicism or conservative ideas about what's considered geeky or sexy, caught on in the West. Unfortunately, most Japanese magazines, known to be exceptionally informative, passed up on English translations, hence remaining, like so many websites today, inaccessible to an international readership.

We have all witnessed, and are still witnessing, exploring, and sharing the incredible accumulation and speedy evolution of digital technologies for documenting, manipulating, publishing, and sharing everyone's individual scoops, opinions, views, and creations. One way or the other, we are now constantly profiling ourselves, even more so in our online universe than offline. What I've learned from my magazine days and from observing the Japanese, is that 'street fashion' and the average level of style thrives spectacularly when there's a critical, appreciative and competitive audience of peers. All these incredibly professional street fashion blogs, like the ones listed in this book, and many more like THE SARTORIALIST, FACE HUNTER, and JAK & JIL, putting all that fashion love out there: I think it's great. 'Great' is an understatement, because it serves the independence of talent as much as it serves the collective eye for style.

Whatever the new wave, quality, authenticity and urgency will always surface. It's a universal law. Now, with open source web, more than ever before. To those who feel threatened in their professional power I would say: you don't have to be the new wave in order to surf it.

ABOUT
Mrs. Mo Veld

Throughout her career, in which fashion and communication played leading roles, Mo Veld became mainly known as a writer. She claims it is due to her art school education in fashion design that she shows more interest in talented people and their ideas, behaviour, workmanship, and ultimately in how this materialises in great brands and products, than in that other side of fashion (where it all seems to evolve around it-bags and celebrities).

www.moveld.com

FAVOURITE BLOGS
www.thesartorialist.blogspot.com
+
www.fantasticman.com
+
www.mykromag.com/blog
+
www.theselby.com
+
www.tmagazine.blogs.nytimes.com

GARANCE DORÉ

Garance Doré's name sounds as classy as her fashion blog looks. The Corsica-born French artist combines her drawings with words, and her words with style photography of the Parisian chic and beautiful. "It's rock and chic at the same time."

In 2006, Garance started her blog to share her thoughts and lovely drawings with the world. "Soon I realised that most of my writings were about fashion. My interest in it is nearly obsessive, and I was inspired by THE SARTORIALIST to expand my blog. Just like he does, I want to show my readers my points of view on fashion." Garance spends most of her time working on her blog. "It's so woven into my daily life that I don't think in terms of blogging or not blogging. I always have my camera with me. So I never go 'hunting', but I just shoot the interesting people that I come across during the day. My blog gives me the opportunity to talk about my jobs as photographer, illustrator, writer, and stylist, and it has lead to many commissions all over the world. I don't make a living with my blog only, but indirectly it generates income, and my professional life would be totally different without it."

GARANCEDORE now has more than 50000 readers per day, though Garance doesn't look at the stats very often. "I sometimes check if my blog is healthy and growing, but when I start thinking about it seriously it's also quite scary to imagine how many people read my words. I like the idea of talking to a friend when I write."

How would you describe your personal style, and does style blogging influence the way you dress?
"My style is very simple. I love greys and blues, pants and cotton T-shirts, and I always wear heels. I love shoes. I'm also crazy about accessories. I have a lot of belts, gloves, and scarves. So I keep it simple, but always try to add a striking detail. Of course, taking pictures of stylish people has refined my eye and the way I dress."

What can you say about French style?
"I love it because it's chic and rock at the same time. A certain kind of deconstructed sophistication, effortless sexiness, at least for the girls. I kind of regret that the Parisian men aren't more daring with their fashion choices."

BLOG TITLE
Garance Doré

URL
www.garancedore.fr

EDITOR
Garance Doré

YEAR OF BIRTH
1975

ONLINE SINCE
June 2006

COUNTRY
France

LANGUAGE
French/English

POSTS PER WEEK
5

VISITORS PER DAY
50000

TAGS
diary, illustration, photography

FAVOURITE BLOGS
www.thesartorialist.blogspot.com
+
www.theselby.com
+
www.fashionologie.com

by Kirstin Hanssen

You opted for a specific approach in taking photos: portrait-style photography, mainly of fashion industry insiders. Why this decision?

"The first time I published a portrait, it was a technical issue, because I thought it would fit better with the format of the other blog images, and I love to have a striking top image. But when I think about it, I believe that I've always wanted to make portraits. One of my projects, when I have time for it, is painting very classical portraits. Besides that, I think that fashion is about the person who wears it. I love to see all that is expressed in a gaze. But I don't picture fashion insiders only! I shoot them during the fashion weeks and of course these people are trained to be stylish, but they are also an inspiration for others to be more daring in everyday life. The rest of the year, it is just people I meet on the street that are in front of my camera."

To what degree are your photos staged and your models styled?

"It depends. At regular street style shootings, I decide what I'm going to do with the background when I meet the person. In some cases I slightly arrange their hair or ask them to open a jacket, or to take the bag off their shoulders. Sometimes, I do a special feature about someone whose style I love. In that case, we take a few hours and talk about the outfits, etc. But it is still very natural, I don't do make-up. I also have my page on VOGUE.FR with the feature 'Une fille, Un Style', which is more intimate portraits of stylish girls."

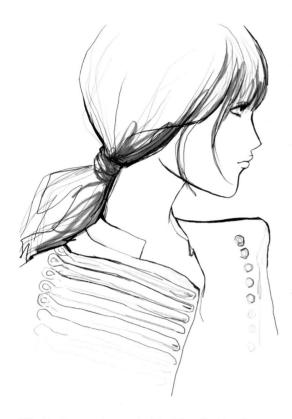

What is the most remarkable thing that has happened since you started blogging?

"Many exciting things happened, and I work in a totally different way now. I'm living my dream to become a fashion photographer, and have my own creative little studio now. Doing photography, illustration, styling, and all kinds of projects. I've been shooting fashion editorials for big name magazines, having photography exhibitions, and I was also asked to make illustrations for GAP's fortieth anniversary pop-up store in London. Furthermore, I met many friends, and I found love!"

Do you think the growing influence of blogging is altering the role of fashion magazines?

"I believe it's pushing the magazines to improve their editing, be more consistent, inspiring and more driven. Nowadays, they can't just publish pictures of fashion shows or products, because all of those have already been on the internet for months. Magazines have to tell a story, build a romance... And a lot of magazines are very good at that! Fashion talk on internet is of a different type. I think that the interaction between printed and online media creates a very stimulating energy."

The number of fashion blogs has exploded. Who will survive?

"Those who have the talent to actually communicate with their audience and have a clear vision on what they are doing. I think that talent will remain. It's also important to actually maintain your blog and to upgrade it to a higher level whenever it is possible."

HEL LOOKS

Liisa Jokinen and Sampo Karjalainen started HEL LOOKS in the summer of 2005, when they realised how colourful and interesting the street style of Helsinki had become. "Helsinkians want to experiment and create their own version of fashion."

"The Japanese photographer Shoichi Aoki and his magazines FRUITS, STREET, and TUNE were a big source of inspiration, and motivated us to start something similar in Finland," explains Liisa Jokinen. "We love fashion, photography, and meeting new people, but we also want to encourage people to dress in an individual way. HEL LOOKS is furthermore a promotional tool for our hometown Helsinki and for Finnish designers. It's purely a hobby project, so it isn't our aim to make a living with it. I earn my salary with freelance writing, and Sampo works as chief creative director at an online entertainment company."

How much time do you spend on your blog?
"It's hard to tell. I carry the camera nearly always with me. Preparing the pictures and updating the site every Sunday takes around two to three hours."

How important are stats for you?
"Of course, it's nice to know that we have many thousands of foreign visitors, but I don't check our stats that often. HEL LOOKS is a passion for us. Meeting new people and getting direct feedback are bigger motivations than statistics."

How would you describe your personal style, and has blogging influenced the way you dress?
"I like second hand and mixing old and new. I like simple clothes with a twist, Finnish and Scandinavian vintage. I either buy used clothes, ecologically sustainable clothes, or invest in quality design pieces. My style was always the same, but since HEL LOOKS, my goal is to look 'hel-lookable' every day! Probably I think about clothes more often than before, but I also have the feeling that I can basically wear anything because anything can look good."

BLOG TITLE
Hel Looks

URL
www.hel-looks.com

EDITORS
Liisa Jokinen,
Sampo Karjalainen

YEAR OF BIRTH
1974, 1977

ONLINE SINCE
July 2005

COUNTRY
Finland

LANGUAGE
English

POSTS PER WEEK
0-10

VISITORS PER DAY
10000

TAGS
helsinki, photography

FAVOURITE BLOGS
www.facehunter.blogspot.com
+
www.stylebubble.co.uk
+
www.thecobrasnake.com

by Kirstin Hanssen

Do you think you inspire other people or set trends with your blog?
"Yes, I do! Personally, fashion blogs inspire me a lot more than fashion magazines, for example."

Why do you think Helsinki kids have such a unique and distinctive style compared to other places worldwide?
"Well, first of all people in Helsinki believe that there are no limitations to what you can wear. I like the fact that the people here are really into fashion, but instead of just copying a style from the catwalk or a magazine, they experiment and create their own version of fashion. Clothes are not status symbols for Helsinkians. Many people truly like shopping and wearing second hand and vintage clothes. Furthermore, I think we Finns want to be individuals. We want to dress up in a relaxed way, which means we are not eager to follow rules. Maybe it's because of our geographical isolation. We are a bit crazy, doing our own thing in many senses!"

Why do you think street style blogs are so successful?
"Blogs are fast and there's a freedom of speech in the blogosphere. Anyone can blog, anyone can create content, and anyone can comment. Blogs generate more impulses and inspiration than fashion magazines."

Do you think the growing influence of blogging is altering the role of fashion magazines?
"Blogs have challenged the role of fashion magazines. Blogs are faster and speed is a factor that is vital to the fashion system."

What is the most remarkable thing that has happened since you started blogging?
"My whole life has changed since we started HEL LOOKS. I quit my daily job and started freelancing, because people got to know me better and I was offered interesting freelance jobs. A big thing was also our exhibition that has been to Denmark, Russia, Estonia, Latvia, Lithuania, Spain, and Germany."

What does the future hold for HEL LOOKS?
"We would like to continue for many years, even for decades. We want to emphasize quality over quantity. Someday, we might stop HEL LOOKS for a month or a year, and then continue again. I regard HEL LOOKS more as a kind of archive than as a project that only lasts for a certain period of time. The longer lifespan this archive covers, the more interesting it is."

STIL IN BERLIN

Mary Scherpe of STIL IN BERLIN is beginning to find out what the complications of being a successful and very busy blogger are. Between working as a photo and fashion editor for UNLIKE.NET and as a fashion consultant/editor for myspace.com/laufsteg, maintaining her blog pudri.blogspot.com and studying art history in addition, she doesn't have as much time to spend on her street style blogging as she would like. Still, Mary explains, the relatively sinking amount of posts isn't 'just' a time-issue, as: "To take pictures that satisfy me takes a lot more time than one year ago, I got pickier with the people I choose and invest more time into quality photography."

This regard for quality over quantity prevails in Mary's vision, as does the idea of doing justice to her beloved city. Rather than simply registering what 'hipster kids' are wearing today, it is capturing the true essence of Berlin that Mary focuses on: "I contribute to the zeitgeist and hopefully my pictures offer a source of inspiration." As it is aptly stated on the blog's front page: "Fashion can describe what a city is, so we take photos of outfits that stand out and capture that spirit."

What can you say about the street style in Berlin?
"I refuse to explain Berlin's style. I don't think there's much sense in trying to find definitions for something that is as changing as fashion."

What is the most remarkable thing that has happened since you started blogging?
"That must be my trips to Paris with CHANEL and to New York with SONY."

Are you in touch with other bloggers?
"Yes, with several. I know a lot of the German fashion bloggers, like F&ART and STYLECLICKER, but also some from Paris like Géraldine Dormoy, Delphine Desneiges and Géraldine Grisey, and Susanna Lau from London."

How important are stats for you?
"STIL IN BERLIN has a quite constant readership that slowly rises. Knowing that there are people who like this project so much, and seeing that they return regularly motivates me."

BLOG TITLE
Stil In Berlin

URL
www.stilinberlin.blogspot.com

EDITORS
Mary Scherpe, Dario Natale

YEAR OF BIRTH
-

ONLINE SINCE
March 2006

COUNTRY
Germany

LANGUAGE
English

POSTS PER WEEK
1

VISITORS PER DAY
2200

TAGS
berlin, fashion

FAVOURITE BLOGS
www.garancedore.fr
+
www.theimagist.com
+
www.whats-wrong-with-the-zoo.de
+
www.thevagabondset.com
+
www. lynnandhorst.blogspot.com

by Elina Tozzi

Why do you think street style blogs are so successful?
"They brought the average pedestrian into the centre of attention."

Do you think the blog world has changed in the past years?
"It's professionalising, and you will not be recognised if you don't stand out now. That means you have to look at any project with professionalism, investing in the quality of photos, choice, and text."

How do you see the future of fashion blogs?
"Regarding street style blogs, I think it will come down to approximately five that offer really good work with excellent photographers behind the project. The competition is getting harder, so just going out and taking a bad picture of someone will not bring you anywhere anymore."

Do you think the growing influence of blogging is altering the role of fashion magazines?
"I hope they'll improve because of the competition. Magazines like INSTYLE Germany publish pictures you can see on the net weeks before, so they face a challenge, but still, good content will lead to success. Online and offline."

COPENHAGEN STREET STYLE

If the ratio between dog years and human years is seven to one, then what constitutes an internet year? In the past decade, this has become a common metaphor used to indicate the internet's fast-pace and continuous evolution. Surely, it can also be applied to the world of street style blogs, which has undergone an entire cycle of being born (around 2005), reaching puberty, and growing into maturity in a relatively short period. Thus, 2009 introduced a new phase, in which the novelty of the genre undeniably waned, and the proverbial cream was separated from the crop. Street style blogs now must feature high-quality photography to be able to stand the test of time, and cannot lack a discerning eye for when the regular and everyday is simply *too* regular.

Looking at COPENHAGEN STREET STYLE, there is no question the bloggers responsible for it apply this critical approach to their photos. Søren Jepsen (1983, Denmark) and Jenny Söderman (1981, Sweden) have established the challenge that maintaining this high quality can pose since they began taking street style photos in early 2007. They explain: "It does get hard to find people after a while because it's always the same people that dress cool. People in small cities also tend to look exactly the same. They buy their clothes in the same stores, go to the same clubs, and all know each other." Søren and Jenny don't think the phenomenon of street style blogs will be dying any time soon, but do predict "there will be a focus on quality instead of quantity." As to the plethora of fashion blogs flooding the web today, they say: "There's so many at the moment, maybe too many. At least when it comes to regular fashion blogs, there's just so many to choose from and the really good ones are few..."

Why did you decide to start COPENHAGEN STREET STYLE?
"COPENHAGEN STREET STYLE is a documentary street style blog with the aim of capturing fashion and what people are wearing at the moment in Copenhagen. We started the blog because we were really sick of the glossy magazines, with their perfect pictures of perfect people in perfect settings with perfect and very expensive clothes. We were both amazed that there really weren't any street style blogs in Copenhagen, and decided to start one of our own."

BLOG TITLE
Copenhagen Street Style

URL
www.copenhagenstreetstyle.dk

EDITORS
Søren Jepsen, Jenny Söderman

YEAR OF BIRTH
1983, 1981

ONLINE SINCE
2007

COUNTRY
Denmark

LANGUAGE
English

POSTS PER WEEK
1-7

VISITORS PER DAY
2500-3500

TAGS
personal style

FAVOURITE BLOGS
www.stylebubble.co.uk
+
www.lesmads.com
+
www.garancedore.fr
+
www.chasejarvis.com/blog

by Elina Tozzi

What can you say about street style in Copenhagen?
"We both think there's been stagnation in Copenhagen for a while now.
There was a lot of focus on crazy colours and prints and oversize cuts a
while ago, and at first that was really exciting and new. But more recently
there has been a shift towards a more tailored look, which the Danish
designers didn't follow at first. I think the designers, the buyers, and the
consumers are ready for something new and it'll be exciting to see the
change. The interest in Swedish designers has grown immensely in
Denmark in the past year and a lot of Swedish brands have opened
flagship-stores in Copenhagen."

Has style blogging influenced the way you dress?
Jenny: "I think it has actually made me less prone to following trends
slavishly. I tend to go for classics, neutral colours, and things that I know
are going to last. Doing this blog has made me realise just how fickle
trends are: they come and go and people spend a lot of money on things
that might last one season, if they're lucky."
Søren: "It has made me more aware of the advantages of each brand,
it has made me more interested in fashion and aware of the fact that
details make all the difference."

Do you think you inspire other people or set trends with your blog?
"We think that street style blogs in general play a huge role in forming
trends. People are interested in what other people are wearing and it's
natural that they get influenced. I don't know if we could be responsible

for any trends though, our job is to pick up on trends that already exist and document them. We don't want to steer people into trends."

Why do you think blogs have become such an important medium?
"Obviously, the web is a lot faster-paced. You can get up-to-the-minute news instantly and there's more of a two-way communication. We believe there's been a shift towards 'reality'. People are more interested in things they can relate to."

Do you think the growing influence of blogging is altering the role of fashion magazines?
"Yes, we believe there's a major power-shift going on. The bloggers are gaining ground and the old hierarchy is being questioned, which is always a good thing. One can find fashion news on the net and on particular blogs faster than the magazines can blink. To survive, I think magazines have to focus on showing more depth in their articles and produce better features and photo-shoots."

people want to see something new

THE STREETS WALKER

It turns out that while fashion's big business is conducted on a very limited number of geographic locations, true style does not obey rules of geography. And while Israel may not be the first place to come to mind when one thinks of (street) style, Yael Sloma, Tel Aviv native, was positive her city did harbour true gems of style. It was not until her trip to one of the world's more established cities of fashion however, that Yael realised the potential of what was right in front of her, and decided to start THE STREETS WALKER, in the beginning of 2007: "I had been following street fashion blogs such as HEL LOOKS, FACE HUNTER, and THE SARTORIALIST for a while. But after I paid a visit to London, I started to understand the importance and the greatness of street fashion, and decided to document it in my city Tel Aviv."

A shift to the everyday

According to Yael, this 'greatness of street fashion' resides mainly in the creativity and individuality that lies at the core of street style. Now, she says, "it is not about how many clothes you have or how much they cost, but about how you put them together." While fashion in the pre-blogging era was, according to Yael, mainly about consumption and expensive designer clothing, fashion today has a different or alternative focus. "Street style blogs put regular people in the spotlight, and make you understand that you can also do it, that everyone can be fashionable." Every*one*, and indeed every*where*: Paris, New York, or Tel Aviv.

The power of blogs

Yael also sees the current shift as possibly having greater effects, as she thinks street style blogging "undermines the fashion industry, creates new beauty forms, and challenges the way we think about fashion." It is the immediacy inherent in the medium of blogs that Yael specifically says poses a threat to the way the fashion industry operates today. As she explains: "Street fashion blogs present the readers with the most avant-garde people from their city. This used to be the role of trend-forecasters, who tried to provide designers with inspiration and marketing tips. Only after two years, the rest of the people wore an adaptation of an adaptation of an adaptation of this avant-garde trend." Now, however, "everyone can see the raw, original form of what the trend could be in three years within only a few hours, on their computer screen. The direct outcome of this may even be the end of seasonal trends as

BLOG TITLE
The Streets Walker

URL
www.thestreetswalker.com

EDITOR
Yael Sloma

YEAR OF BIRTH
1987

ONLINE SINCE
March 2007

COUNTRY
Israel

LANGUAGE
English, Hebrew

POSTS PER WEEK
5-7

VISITORS PER DAY
–

TAGS
photography

FAVOURITE BLOGS
www.garancedore.fr
+
www.thesartorialist.blogspot.com
+
www. jakandjil.com
+
www. glamcanyon.blogspot.com

by Elina Tozzi

we see it today." The power that blogs and the people who create them have in fashion isn't always fully acknowledged yet, although "people and the media are being more and more respectful to bloggers than they were in the past." But, THE STREETS WALKER concludes: "The big step will be when it won't be surprising when someone writes under profession: 'a blogger'."

THE STREETHEARTS

THE STREETHEARTS, started in March 2009, is the new shooting star in the universe of street style blogs. Co-founder Eirik Slyngstad is a freelance photographer, and his partner in crime Andreas Schjønhaug works in web design and usability. This probably also explains the high quality of the blog and its portraits, which are perfectly matched to their environment. A chat with Eirik Slyngstad, who informs us: "We're not robots with cameras!"

What is the most remarkable thing that has happened since you started blogging?
"We've had a lot of international attention from blogs, magazines, newspapers, and we even sold pictures to CONDÉ NAST and BURBERRY. So far, everything has gone so much better than expected!"

Scandinavians are known for their great taste in fashion and their stylishness. How would you describe 'the Scandinavian look'?
"Black... When you walk around on the streets of Copenhagen, Stockholm, and Oslo, you see a lot of women and men dressed in black. They use varieties in volume and structure to shape their outfits in an interesting way. Plain is another way to describe Scandinavian style. So call it dark, sculptural, but plain."

What trends are you sick of, and wouldn't shoot anymore if you saw it on the street?
"I think I wouldn't photograph anyone wearing a lot of studs or sequins. Besides that, I don't appreciate fur, so I'm not really stalking furry people with my camera."

Who would you most like to capture in a photograph?
"Tavi, the teenage style genius. I would love to do a long post featuring her different styles. Charles Guislain is definitely on my list as well. Nothing is more inspiring than young fresh fashion talent!"

Being a professional photographer, do you think you have a different approach than street style bloggers that are foremost bloggers/fashionistas/writers?
"As a photographer you notice things that others usually aren't aware of, and you're able to make an outfit look amazing by taking a great shot.

BLOG TITLE
The Streethearts

URL
www.thestreethearts.com

EDITORS
Andreas Schjønhaug,
Eirik Slyngstad

YEAR OF BIRTH
1981, 1990

ONLINE SINCE
2009

COUNTRY
Norway

LANGUAGE
English

POSTS PER WEEK
2-3

VISITORS PER DAY
2000

TAGS
personal style

FAVOURITE BLOGS
www.theones2watch.com
+
www.tavi-thenewgirlintown.
blogspot.com

by Kirstin Hanssen

I always think 'how can I make this outfit look even better?' By using the right angles, lenses, light directions, and colour corrections, you're able to breathe life into even the most boring jersey dress. And last but not least, being a good communicator to the subjects makes a big difference."

With the huge number of style blogs (and fashion blogs in general), do you get a sense of overkill?
"Andreas and I trust in ourselves and believe that we have a special point of view that people find interesting. I don't think you can really get enough of good street style blogs anyway. The only thing I do find really tedious is all the street style blogs posting the same outfits during fashion week. So instead of taking as many pictures as possible during the fashion weeks, we spend time with each of our subjects to make them feel more comfortable about being photographed. We're not robots with cameras!"

Travelling, making intimate portraits of complete strangers… You must gather a lot of insight on human behaviour. What have you discovered?
"Do you know how everyone on the street seems to be super busy; rushing along all the time? That's what Andreas and I noticed when we first started, so we tried to take the shots in the least amount of time to avoid holding up anyone. But then we realised that most people we photograph actually really don't mind. On the contrary, they take it as a huge compliment that some stranger wants to take their portrait and is interested in what they're wearing. They put effort in their outfit, so when someone notices that they're delighted!"

How do people respond when you mention you are a blogger?
"When we approach people on the street, we actually always introduce ourselves as photographers for a fashion website, as I have the impression that a lot of people don't appreciate the blogging phenomenon, mostly because of all of the thirteen-year-old bloggers who post pictures of themselves in their daily dull outfits."

How do you think the growing influence of blogging is altering the role of fashion magazines?
"I believe all the blogs around the world inspire people to become more style-conscious and also to make fashion more appealing to them. So from that point of view, a person who would never have bought a fashion magazine in the past will now at least consider picking one up. On the other hand, blogs are often started by ordinary people like you and me, and that makes them more real and effective for a large number of readers than magazines do. I think the blogging phenomenon is taking over the fashion world, definitely."

What are your plans for the future?
"I'm moving to New York really soon, and will continue street style photography there, along with my internship with an elite fashion photographer. We are also looking for a third photographer for the blog, based in Paris, Milan, London, or any other interesting city."

PERSONAL STYLE DIARIES

PERSONAL STYLE DIARIES

An enormous amount of factors determine what you are wearing right now. Most are simply practical. You can wear nothing but your handmade leather string bikini to a fetish party in the harbour, but if you wear it to Christmas dinner your mother will probably never speak to you again, or even worse - she will ask to borrow it. Another example: you wouldn't want to be wearing your invaluable hand-painted Alexander McQueen shoulder pads when you're meeting up with that friend of yours that talks while she eats. On the other hand, there are also an enormous amount of practical factors that can lead to you not wearing any clothes at all. It either involves skinny dipping, an uncontrollable carnal desire, or vestiphobia, which is the fear of clothing. (I wanted to put some random trivia in this introduction, and now that I've got that out of the way, let's continue, shall we?)

When it comes to style, an important factor in what you're wearing is whether your body can 'pull something off' or not. A runway model may undoubtedly look great in a piece of exquisite yellow knitwear, but there's a good chance you'd be walking around in it looking like a sad lemon. But: the biggest style influence on your wardrobe of all is the taste of the people whose opinion you respect. Those in your immediate environment are the ones that have to look at your clothes most of the time - not you, unless you're an objectophile and married to a mirror - so you'd have to be quite selfish to wear stuff the people in your environment think is boring or ugly, right? And if there are fashion bloggers whose style you admire, you're probably already copying them. My point is: the most important influence on your wardrobe never seems to be you yourself. Which reminds me of someone.

Back in high school, there was this girl in my class named Nathalie. She was really cute and cheerful, and could easily have been the most popular girl in school. She wasn't, because she wore handkerchiefs as dresses. Not because she was poor and her parents had to dress her in old snot cloths: she would sew them herself and wear them simply because she liked them. She said she thought it was important to wear stuff she really loved, rather than wearing the clothing societal influences told her to wear. In short, she didn't give a shit about what other people thought. So of course I teased her. Independent thought in high school? Come on.

Everyone should know by now that throughout these last couple of years, the fashion environment has undergone some serious landscaping, because the blogosphere made a more personal approach to fashion possible. Fashion magazine editors were both replaced and heavily influenced by personal bloggers: people who tied their love for fashion to their internet connections, and started garnishing fashion news with their personal views, serving it to everybody who wanted to eat it. The traditional media are still losing ground to opinionated, sometimes even sceptical fashion bloggers that aren't afraid to speak out against some of the biggest and usually unconditionally respected players in the fashion world. Their personal touch is what makes their opinions easy to relate to: they show us that fashion is about you, and no one else, really.

In retrospect, that cute girl in my class was quite the hero, of course. Everybody should wear sown-together handkerchiefs, if that is what they want to wear. You shouldn't need a designer, fashion magazine, or even a blogger to tell you that it's

by Marten Mantel

okay to. This girl was on to something. So: I'm sorry, Nathalie. Both for misjudging you and for sneezing in your dresses all those times.

ABOUT
Marten Mantel

As a writer and journalist, Marten Mantel has been free-lancing quite randomly through the Dutch print and online magazine world. He previously wrote for Dutch newspaper NRC.NEXT and was the copy editor of online youth medium SPUNK. He is currently the online editor and copy editor of VICE MAGAZINE NL. He knows more about blogging than about fashion, though he is the proud owner of an impressive collection of velours sweaters.

www.wijkunnenschrijvengoed.nl

FAVOURITE BLOGS
www.robbiebaauw.blogspot.com
+
www.vicestyle.com
+
www.thecatorialist.blogspot.com

SEA OF SHOES

SEA OF SHOES is paradise for those with a zest for high heels, designer wear, and vintage pieces, in other words: for just about every woman on the planet. "I was always shy, but I felt much more confident in good shoes," explains blogger Jane Aldridge.

January 2010: Jane Aldridge is featured in the Bright Young Things section of VANITY FAIR. Not bad for someone who is in her last year of high school and claims to have started blogging out of sheer boredom. The beloved Jane says: "I first began in the spring of 2007, but quickly got disinterested as it was a lot of work. A year later, I started it up again, and since then I've been blogging regularly. After a few months I was approached by URBAN OUTFITTERS, to design a shoe line for them. A surprise, since my blog didn't have such a wide readership back then. I was very thrilled, and enjoyed learning about the manufacturing process. I would love to design shoes again in the future." Jane's mother is designer and socialite Judy Aldridge, a fellow blogger. "My mom and I photograph each other often for our blogs. I'm lucky to have very supportive parents. Even though the path that I've taken isn't a conventional one, they've embraced my choices and kept a really open mind. My mom is so knowledgeable about fashion and she's a great inspiration. Because of her I've become very passionate about collecting vintage couture."

What is it like living in Trophy Club, Texas?
"Trophy Club is a quiet, conservative suburban town. I go to Dallas pretty often though. Texas is full of eccentrics. So much of Texas is very desolate and isolated, so it's easy for people to retreat into their own little obsessive worlds. In a way, it's a very dark and depressing place, but I enjoy the solitude most of the time. Texas likes flash and isn't afraid to be gaudy. I'm definitely drawn to gaudy!"

How would your style differ if you had grown up in New York or Paris?
"If I would have grown up there, I'm not sure, but I'd probably be much more jaded. I find Paris and NYC a little overstimulating in terms of fashion, as everything is available to you! Living in Texas means you have to look hard to find what you like. I enjoy the hunt. Oh, and I probably wouldn't get such great deals on shoes and clothes! Here we have great thrifting and amazing shoe sales."

BLOG TITLE
Sea of Shoes

URL
www.seaofshoes.com

EDITOR
Jane Aldridge

YEAR OF BIRTH
1991

ONLINE SINCE
2008

COUNTRY
USA

LANGUAGE
English

POSTS PER WEEK
3-4

VISITORS PER MONTH
275000

TAGS
shoes, style, vintage

FAVOURITE BLOGS
www. dandygum.blogspot.com
+
www.fashionispoison.com
+
www.thatschic.net

by Kirstin Hanssen

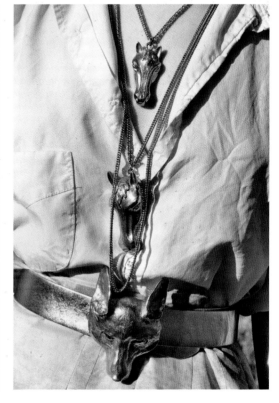

Having what you might call an expensive taste, how do you finance all of your purchases, and what particular item would you buy if money were no object?

"I'd rather not answer the first part of that question, and if money were no object, I'd buy a dress from YSL's 1976 Russian collection."

Have you always had this 'obsession' with shoes?

"When I was younger and couldn't wear women's shoes yet, I remember always going to NEIMAN MARCUS with my mom and watching her pick out those killer 90's PRADA kitten heels. She had these spotted pony hair buckle kitten heels that I was obsessed with. I was very excited when I first started wearing heels. They make you feel very powerful! I was always shy, but I felt much more confident in good shoes."

Talking about heels... do your feet ever ache?

"No, I've pretty much deformed my feet to the point where they can stand anything. No pain, no gain. Maybe I'm a masochist."

Why did you decide to disable comments on SEA OF SHOES, seeing that you received so many?

"I didn't see the necessity of comments on a personal blog. It's a little creepy to invite people to say whatever they want about you. And reading them every day makes you feel like an absolute lunatic. I'm much happier without them. I used to get some very strange ones, and they made me very uncomfortable, even though the vast majority of them were very sweet."

How do you think the world of fashion blogs has changed in the past years?

"The number of fashion blogs has increased exponentially: it seems like everyone has one now. People are definitely beginning to take fashion and style blogs more seriously, but I don't think any of us is sure what it will all end up leading to. It's been very exciting to watch!"

ELINKAN

Some girls seem to be born with style in their genes. Somehow, they always look flawless; they never even have a bad hair day. One of those girls is Swedish Elin Jönsson, born in 1990. This pretty blonde adores red lipstick, dresses, and high heels. Her blog ELINKAN shows us dream-like scenery, its beautiful photos often made by Elin's younger sister.

"ELINKAN is what my aunt used to call me when I was a little girl. I started my blog about a year after I started reading blogs. I wanted to inspire people, the same thing as others did for me. I wanted to blog about clothes, fashion, and things that I like," Elin explains. Blogging occupies an important role in her daily life, and she considers her blog as her baby. "I want to take care of it, and make it as good as I can. I only post what I'm a 100% satisfied with and only when I have enough time to prepare it. Sometimes it takes just half an hour to come up with a great idea or to make that special picture, but it can also take a couple of hours. Most of the time I come up with an idea, and my little sister of fourteen takes my photos. Then I edit them. It has always been like that, and it's great because we are such a wonderful team. My blog wouldn't be the same without her!" When looking at ELINKAN, one wonders who lives in this fairytale world: the real Elin, or her alter ego. "It's me who lives in that world, or me who wishes she did. In the tiny village where I live, everything can look like a fairytale. There's a silent lake and there are big, strangely shaped trees."

Recognised on the street

Elin's blog attracts up to 3500 visitors per day, but statistics are less important for the bright-eyed blogger than the readers commenting on her inspiring outfits are. It also occurred that she was recognised on the street. "Some people have even said 'hi' to me and that they like my blog. It feels a bit weird that strangers know who I am, but at the same time it's flattering. No, I have never received any strange comments or mails and so on. Maybe it's because I don't write very much about personal things, or maybe I've just been lucky."

Old-fashioned with a modern touch

Looking at ELINKAN, we feel a bit jealous of how Elin manages to wear even the most retro, old-fashioned dresses, without ever looking frumpy. "How I would describe my personal style? I think it's cute, but maybe

BLOG TITLE
Elinkan

URL
www.radarzine.com/blogg/elinkan

EDITOR
Elin Jönsson

YEAR OF BIRTH
1990

ONLINE SINCE
January 2007

COUNTRY
Sweden

LANGUAGE
Swedish & English

POSTS PER WEEK
6-7

VISITORS PER DAY
3000-3500

TAGS
feminine, exquisite, extraordinary

FAVOURITE BLOGS
www.folkbladet.nu/?cat=89
+
www.rodeo.net/niotillfem
+
www. quietland.blogg.se

by Kirstin Hanssen

also a bit old-fashioned with a modern touch. I like to mix patterns and colours and to wear lipstick! My blog did influence the way I dress: I'm more experimental than I was in the beginning. My philosophy of dressing is that everyone can look great in anything, as long as they feel comfortable in it."

A design of her own
According to Elin the future for fashion and style blogs looks bright. "I always need to be inspired, and I think everyone has the urge for that. Blogs are fun and make us creative. My own future plans are not defined yet. My blog could probably be a step-up to working in the fashion industry, but I don't know exactly what I want to do to make a living. One thing I do know for sure is that I need a creative job. Right now I think that I'd like to become some kind of designer."

RENÉE STURME

In a tiny town in the south of The Netherlands, far, far away from the world's booming metropolises, a wide-eyed, somewhat bored girl spent her days walking alongside the village river, listening to the birds sing, and dreaming of the day her real life would begin. Her love for unique vintage clothing making her somewhat of an eccentric in her town, Renée Sturme revelled in the thought of one day being able to live in the big city, where she could explore her true self and dance the night away with her fashion-minded friends. In the meantime, she decided to start a blog, FASHION FILLERS (now simply RENÉESTURME/BLOG), where she could share her passions with a few others. As it turned out, blogging was just what this girl needed to get her creative juices flowing. Her professional juices, too: besides landing a job at a vintage shop through her blog, Renée also launched her very own online boutique, selling vintage and self-made jewellery. Suffice it to say Renée isn't bored much anymore.

Why did you decide to start a blog?

"One day, I just had the urge to connect with others that shared my interests, as they had never really been around in my actual life, so I started my blog. Now, my blog's still just really personal, it's about what I wear, things I find and adore on the internet (from a pair of heels to a great street style picture), photography that shows bits of my daily life, and random stuff I feel like sharing. "

What influence has living in a small town had on you and on your blog?

"To know how to appreciate things others see as normal or even annoying. To value the noise of cars on the road, or even the smell of public transportation, just because then you know there's life on the streets.
The positive part isn't as big as the downside, however. There's nothing to do in my hometown, so I haven't been able to experience - for example – nightlife in the city, which can be a big part of creating your personality. I don't really know how it influenced my blogging. Readers may like the fact I live in a so-called cosy and picturesque place, because they might live in the city. You always want what you can't have."

What is typically Dutch about you?

"Possibly being more down to earth, though at the same time I can also be quite the critic. I don't feel typically Dutch in any way actually, so this

BLOG TITLE
renéesturme/blog

URL
www.fashionfillers.com

EDITOR
Renée Sturme

YEAR OF BIRTH
1991

ONLINE SINCE
May 2007

COUNTRY
The Netherlands

LANGUAGE
English

POSTS PER WEEK
20

VISITORS PER DAY
2000-3000

TAGS
photography, vintage

FAVOURITE BLOGS
www.fashiontoast.com
+
www.amlul.com
+
www.fashionsquad.com

by Elina Tozzi

is quite hard to answer. I think I'm more a resident of the World than a resident of The Netherlands."

What's the most remarkable thing that has happened since you started blogging?
"Because of having a blog, people notice you more. Thanks to blogging I now have a wonderful job at a vintage web shop, which is a big part of my life. Another way is people actually recognising you on the street, and being invited to fashion shows."

Why did you decide to start your jewellery line and would you consider it for a future career?
"I've always been making jewellery, since being about eight years old, and this year I just took the step to actually do something with it. So I created myself a little web shop. I love that people appreciate my creations because making jewellery is one of my favourite things to do. It will always be a part of my life, but probably more as an expanded hobby than a real career."

What would you have been spending your time on if you had grown up without the internet?
"To be honest, I really don't have a clue. I wouldn't be able to work at a web shop, I wouldn't be able to sell my jewellery all over the world, etc. My life would probably have been quite boring!"

What are your future plans?
"My goal is to study photography at an art academy, but I'm still working out my ideas and creating my personal style. What's currently important to me is moving to Amsterdam, whether I'm going to study there or not. I hope I will discover myself even more there."

MODERNITETER

MODERNITETER is the blog of two true Swedish darlings, sisters Olivia and Amanda Åkerman. They show us daily glimpses of their life, and their ever-inspiring wardrobe. These girls, however, are not aiming at setting trends, and in fact think "trends are pretty boring." Although the blog, mainly written in Swedish, contains numerous pictures of the girls in their latest outfits, they don't even consider themselves 'style addicts'. "We're not that into fashion, we just like to wear nice clothes. We get inspired by people we see in the streets, and by our friends."

When asked to describe MODERNITETER, they explain: "Our blog is about ourselves, how we are spending our days and nights, about our friends and things we like or dislike. Moderniteter means modernity, something new. That's what we at least try to be." But just because MODERNITETER has the sisters' daily life as its topic, that sure doesn't mean they will share every detail of it: "We don't write anything that is too personal. Not only because we have so many readers, but also since it will be on the internet forever."

What does MODERNITETER mean to you in your daily life?
"Blogging has become a natural part of our lives. We almost always carry a camera with us, and we often think of things that we want to blog about or photos that we want to post."

What is the most remarkable thing that has happened since you started blogging?
"We have been doing photo shoots, both as models, stylists, and photographers. Last winter we were involved in designing a jewellery collection for a Swedish brand called MILAJKI. But the best thing is that we had the chance to meet all the wonderful new people!"

How important are stats for you?
"We try not to look at the stats too often, because it shouldn't be how many readers you have that is important. When we first started blogging we never thought that it would grow so big. We would probably blog even if we only had five readers, but maybe not as regular as we do now."

Where exactly do you live in Sweden and does this influence your blog?
"We live in a small town called Frillesås, situated fifty kilometres south

BLOG TITLE
Moderniteter

URL
www.modette.se/moderniteter/
blogg

EDITORS
Olivia & Amanda Åkerman

YEAR OF BIRTH
1989, 1991

ONLINE SINCE
August 2006

COUNTRY
Sweden

LANGUAGE
Swedish / English

POSTS PER WEEK
20

VISITORS PER DAY
5000

TAGS
patterns, pop

FAVOURITE BLOGS
www.rodeo.net/lisa-corneliusson
+
www.elle.se/filippa-bergs-blogg.
aspx
+
www.olfa.blogg.se
+
www.majpaj.blogspot.com

by Kirstin Hansen

of Gothenburg, a big town on the Swedish west coast. Most kids around here only play football, but we hate sports, so we had to find something else to spend our time on. So no, we can't say that it has really influenced us, but the blog is more like an opposite reaction to it."

How would you describe your personal style?
Our styles are quite similar sometimes, but they change from day to day. It would be wrong to describe it as classic, cute, grunge, fashion, bohemian, or whatever, because it is a mix of so many styles. We wear a lot of second hand clothes and match it with our grandmother's old clothes, new stuff, pink boots, a lot of striped T-shirts, floral prints, and ex-boyfriends' old clothes, among other things!"

Do you think you inspire other people with MODERNITETER or set trends with it?
"We sure hope that we can inspire people, but to set trends is not really something we aim for, since we think that trends are pretty boring. But it's a subtle line between inspiring people and creating trends. Our surroundings affect us all the time, and we guess that our blog also affects at least some people, and by that we might have set some trends with it."

Talking about affecting people... have you ever received any strange or unsettling reactions?
"Actually, we have been spared from that. We get bitter comments almost every day, but there is never anybody who is actually mean. But when we were in Copenhagen, some Swedish girls who stayed at the same hotel as us shouted our names when they passed by on the street. That felt kind of strange."

Do you think this kind of style blogging is a specific 'girl thing', or do you also know boys who do it?
"We only know a few boys who are interested in clothes and fashion, and who also blog about it. It is much more common that girls do it, probably because a blog can be like an online diary and diary writing often is seen as a girly thing to do. That's a shame, since it is such a great way to express yourself and to remember things that happened."

How do you see the future of fashion blogs?
"We think that the fashion blog movement has reached its peak. It will probably keep on going this well for a couple more years, but then people will be tired of it and look to other sources for inspiration. Blogs in general will not go away, because they are a new and important part of the media culture."

- always looking for new

PANDORA

Art history student Louise Ebel has beauty, brains, and a fascination for the 19th century. "I'm writing a memoir about women's constrained bodies in that age, but I am also really into its decadence and *la vie de bohème*." Welcome to the world of PANDORA.

What does the name PANDORA represent to you?
"It refers to Greek mythology, as I am really interested in Pandora, one of the first *femme fatales* and an early example of misogyny and the general fear for women. But the main reason I named the blog PANDORA is that she is more or less my alter ego, it's not me exactly."

What is the secret behind your success?
"I guess it's my mix of fashion and art, it's different."

Are you working as a model or do you aspire to do so?
"No, and I don't have that ambition. I just like to express my tastes via photographs. Being a model is different because then you are not the 'art director' of the photo shoot. As I am often asked by people to model for them, it's more like being a 'muse', even if that sounds a bit pretentious."

Your photos do look amazing! Does it take forever to take them?
"I don't take my own pictures, as I'm really bad at it. So I work with photographers who I contact when I have an idea for a photo shoot, or they contact me by showing their work and ideas via FACEBOOK, for example. When we do an editorial-like photo shoot, it usually takes half a day."

You receive so many comments. How do you deal with the negative ones?
"I hardly get negative comments, though some people say that I'm cold and pretentious. It's just because I'm shy and anxious. Most of the time I receive wonderful comments. That encourages me a lot."

What would you like to do after graduating?
"I want to do a Master's degree, write another memoir, and publish my first one as a book. I expect I will continue my blog, because it means a lot to me to express myself through it."

BLOG TITLE
Pandora

URL
www.misspandora.fr

EDITOR
Louise Ebel

YEAR OF BIRTH
1988

ONLINE SINCE
June 2008

COUNTRY
France

LANGUAGE
French / English

POSTS PER WEEK
1-2

VISITORS PER DAY
1000

TAGS
expressive, poetic, creative

FAVOURITE BLOGS
www.thecherryblossomgirl.com
+
www.tendances-de-mode.com
+
www.garancedore.fr

by Kirstin Hanssen

photos by Adeline Mai

CINDIDDY

Cindy Ko is quite the globetrotter. Only in her early twenties, Cindy has already lived in Vancouver, Hong Kong, and Shanghai, and modeled in all of those places, as well as London, starting at the tender age of thirteen. Now working as an assistant creative director and modeling on the side, Cindy, also known by her online name CINDIDDY, says she aspires to work in the fashion industry. "I think a lot about having my own fashion label, starting an online shop to sell vintage clothing and new brands that have yet to be discovered," she muses, and says she also hopes to excel in writing, much alike that *other* famous fashion blogger of Asian descent ("Susie Bubble's writing is absolutely inspiring"). As the countless comments posted on her blog show, fashion fans from all around the globe love to gush over Cindy's luscious photos that reveal Cindy has a strong penchant for all things black, sleek, and chic. And heels, lots and lots of heels.

Why did you start CINDIDDY?

"About a year or two ago, while reading the usual VOGUE, ELLE, etc., I would see these features about 'real' people and fashion blogs. I had no idea what these 'fashion blogs' were, until I saw my sister Shirley reading FASHION TOAST and was hooked instantly. Everything about it, especially seeing the daily decisions these people made, was so interesting and inspiring to me. I already had a blog that I barely updated, but I knew that creating a fashion blog was perfect for me, as fashion has always been important to me."

Why did you choose the name CINDIDDY?

"The name of the blog was important to me because I felt that it would bring out the whole 'feel' of my style and my personality. After a few weeks of thinking about different names, I thought of a nickname my friend Kate gave me, CINDIDDY, which was perfect. It represented me well, as I am fairly traditional with a bit of an edge."

What role does fashion blogging occupy in your daily life?

"Blogging or not, I spend a lot of my free time devoted to fashion, whether it's shopping, reading fashion magazines, fashion sites, DIY-ing, or daydreaming about my own fashion label. Blogging is just a small part of what I love and do. It's a platform for me to share my findings and work, but the reward is much greater."

BLOG TITLE
Cindiddy

URL
www.cindiddy.com

EDITOR
Cindy Ko

YEAR OF BIRTH
1986

ONLINE SINCE
November 2008

COUNTRY
Hong Kong

LANGUAGE
English

POSTS PER WEEK
1-2

VISITORS PER DAY
1000

TAGS
inspiration, passion

FAVOURITE BLOGS
www.stylebubble.co.uk
+
www.sincerelyjules.blogspot.com
+
www.lefashionimage.blogspot.com
+
www.luxirare.com

by Elina Tozzi

What is the most remarkable thing that has happened since you started blogging?

"The comments are remarkable, knowing that these people actually take the time to look at my blog and comment is an amazing feeling in itself. Aside from that, it's the offers I get because of this blog, from writing brand stories for new labels to getting approached to take part in designing, it's all very exciting and absolutely insane."

How is the blogging scene in Hong Kong?

"A lot of my friends who read my blog think it's interesting and they tend to appreciate it. For some, blogging has become a part of their lifestyle, and I know a few people that have also started blogging because of my blog, whether it is personal or about something they love, like food, fashion, etc. The internet has no boundaries, so in Hong Kong as any-where around the world, blogging is something that will only become more popular."

Do you think that fashion blogs are more interesting and inspiring than fashion magazines?

"I think that fashion blogs are a great way to discover individual style. It's inspiration that is more realistic. Like anything, it's easier to learn from people you can relate to. Fashion magazines feed our hunger for things that are more out of reach, They are still inspiring and definitely interesting."

What kind of reader do you envision when you are writing your blog?

"Fashion lovers of course, but sometimes I envision a girl or a boy with magazine pages all around their room. Clothes ripped apart and put back together. DIY clothing or materials lying around, ready to start a new project. Even people at work, secretly clicking through pages of my blog, planning and daydreaming (like me) to one day have a fashion label of their own. I see myself in the readers I envision."

NIOTILLFEM

NIOTILLFEM is perfection. From its creator Sandra Beijer, to her boy-friend Ludvig, to the food they prepare, parties they host, trips they take, and, of course, the clothes they wear: every single aspect of the world of NIOTILLFEM (which means 'nine to five') is absolute and utter perfection. It is this which attracts thousands of people from all over the world to the page. "They are kind, sweet, and often in love with some Pete Doherty-esque guy who once kissed them at a party," the young Swede says about her readers. "They dream of small apartments in Paris, rooftops in New York, and pink dresses with cigarette stains on them."

People seek other, more glamorous worlds beside the one they inhabit, and they find it right here. NIOTILLFEM manages to evoke a certain old world glamour and sophistication, and it's hardly a mystery where Sandra finds her inspiration: "I love the fifties and sixties, puffy skirts, head-bands, and bows. A young Marianne Faithful and Catherine Deneuve, girls like that inspire me a lot." What Sandra enjoys most about blogging is sharing those specific tastes with her readers, and getting acquainted with like-minded people: "What I like is a certain kind of person finding my blog. People that like the same things I do, read the books I read, and also wear polka-dot skirts and also have a soft spot for bunnies."

When asked whether she thinks she inspires others with her blog, Sandra hesitantly says: "I *hope* I inspire people. I write a lot about love and being a teenager and a lot of girls mail me every day and tell me their problems, asking for advice. It makes me feel important as a blogger, because if they take the step to actually email me, a girl they don't even know, they must really need someone to talk to. And I try to help them best I can." It's easy to forget that Sandra is in fact a real person, as her world looks right out of a movie. But perhaps it is precisely this aspect of realness that attracts people to (fashion) blogs in general. "I think people are more interested in personalities than in fashion per se," Sandra comments. Sure, we enjoy seeing improbably skinny models in designer clothes that no one can afford in lighting that will conceal anything that doesn't fit the script, but maybe we would rather know how *real* people look and think, and how they incorporate fashion into their daily lives. Bearing NIOTILLFEM in mind, one might also ask: who needs fiction when reality can look this good?

by Elina Tozzi

BLOG TITLE
Niotillfem

URL
www.rodeo.net/niotillfem

EDITOR
Sandra Beijer

YEAR OF BIRTH
1984

ONLINE SINCE
2005

COUNTRY
Sweden

LANGUAGE
Swedish / English

POSTS PER WEEK
15

VISITORS PER DAY
8000

TAGS
checkers, polka-dots, stripes

FAVOURITE BLOGS
www.blog.krisatomic.com
+
www.thecherryblossomgirl.com
+
www.folkbladet.nu/?cat=89

When clicking through the pages of Sandra's blog, however, you do start to wonder. Or is it perhaps a perfectly staged world, where those things that don't fit in are simply filtered out? To apply the question to the blogosphere in general: do blogs truly grant us a window into people's everyday lives, or is there another reality behind this reality that still remains unseen? It is not a question easily answered, but an interesting one nonetheless. To apply the question to NIOTILLFEM, one could point out that all of Sandra's friends are in creative professions (and likely to be oriented toward the visual), and in this specific case it may thus simply be a matter of milieu. Curious, we ask Sandra whether everyone in Sweden really looks this good, or whether it is indeed to do with her specific group of friends. The platinum blonde, seemingly unaware of the movie-like quality of the world she considers to be so normal, responds: "It's my friends! We are the prettiest, most well-dressed crowd in the world."

LIEBEMARLENE VINTAGE

Rhiannon Leifheit never intended to become one of fashion blogging's vintage darlings. When she started her blog LIEBEMARLENE VINTAGE in the summer of 2007, it was merely meant as a means of promoting her main activity, selling clothes and accessories on EBAY. Soon enough however, she discovered that blogging offered her a creative outlet. As Rhiannon explains: "It's mainly about what's inspiring me at the moment - I post outfit photos as well as inspiration collages. Lots of classic movie photos too." Even now, with 5000-plus visits a day and features in several national magazines, Rhiannon admits that popularity and visitor stats aren't exactly her top priority: "I'm not really a numbers kind of a person, and honestly the comments I get motivate me much more than stats could." Step back in time and indulge in the dreamy retro-ness of LIEBEMARLENE VINTAGE.

What does the title of your blog represent?
"It's actually kind of embarrassing since it was my AOL instant messenger screen name from my college days. It has to do with my old Marlene Dietrich obsession and also my obsession with the German language."

What role does blogging occupy in your daily life?
"I love it, but it's a lot of work, for sure. I'm constantly trying to come up with ideas for posts. It's hard to separate my real life from my blog at this point, as I'm always writing about my personal life and trying to figure out ways to tie the blogging and actual worlds together."

Would you say your EBAY shop now supports your blogging activities or does your blog promote your shop?
"I think that my blog supports my EBAY shop - it's probably where most of my EBAY hits come from, at least. When I started out blogging, I tried to keep my posts completely EBAY-related but at this point I'm probably just as much invested in my blog as I am in my EBAY store."

How would you describe your personal style, and how has blogging influenced the way you dress?
"My personal style is pretty vintage-based and old-fashioned, and I think it's become even more so after reading all the different blogs out there that are written by like-minded people. Blogging definitely makes me want to put a little more effort into my outfits, especially if I'll be

BLOG TITLE
Liebemarlene Vintage

URL
www.liebemarlene.blogspot.com

EDITOR
Rhiannon Leifheit

YEAR OF BIRTH
1980

ONLINE SINCE
July 2007

COUNTRY
USA

LANGUAGE
English

POSTS PER WEEK
5

VISITORS PER DAY
5000

TAGS
classic film, vintage

FAVOURITE BLOGS
www.thecherryblossomgirl.com
+
www.misspandora.fr
+
www.bloomingleopold.blogspot.com
+
www.blushingambition.blogspot.com
+
www.turnedout.tv
+
www.vagabondiana.blogspot.com

by Elina Tozzi

photos by Drew Tyndell

photographing them for the blog. I certainly pay closer attention to details now."

Where did your fascination with vintage clothing and lifestyle come from?
"I've been into vintage for as long as I've been into fashion, but I think that at the beginning it was more out of necessity than anything else. I wasn't particularly interested in actual vintage back then… I had a harder time finding it, but since then it has become a lot easier. I found out that it wasn't all that difficult or expensive to track down clothes that are very similar to the clothes worn by my favourite stars in my favourite classic films."

Do you think you inspire other people with your blog or set trends with it?
"It's hard to say… I think that all of us in the blogging world inspire each other in different ways. I don't really see myself as a trendsetter though, I think my style is too old-fashioned for that!"

You expose a great deal of personal information and thereby put yourself out there for the world to see and possibly judge.
Have you ever received any scary, strange or unsettling reactions?
"I've actually received scarier messages on my FLICKR account than through blogging. I've been fortunate on my blog so far. Most of the people commenting are nicer than I ever thought fashion-minded girls could be."

How do you see the future of fashion blogs?
"I think that they will gain even more influence than they have at the moment and that a lot of the big fashion bloggers will be offered jobs in the magazine world. If anything, I think that blogs are going to shake up the magazines a bit. People read fashion blogs not only for the photos and information they provide, but also for the personalities behind them. Fashion magazines are going to have to become more personal and less distant in order to keep up."

THE STYLISH WANDERER

In the world of fashion blogging, age isn't quite what it used to be. Now, twelve is the starter-age, seventeen is the new twenty, and at twenty-five, well... you're over the hill. Therefore, at fourteen, THE STYLISH WANDERER isn't even nearly the youngest of fashion bloggers. Don't expect the perky brunette to be as naive as her age might lead you to believe either: this teen chooses to keep her real name and home-town hidden 'for safety reasons'. Luckily, it turns out this Wanderer isn't yet done being a kid, her blog being all about finding your true self and true style, and about dreaming of what the future might bring, like being able to experience fashion week in person (rather than via the computer screen). But one step at a time: first, she will be taking on an institution of a different order: High School.

Why did you decide to remain anonymous on your blog and how much editing does it require?
"Being anonymous is strictly for safety reasons. Also, my name has nothing to do with what I wear, which sort of gives me freedom. And it's unnecessary information. I used to have a black bar over my eyes, which you can see in earlier posts on my blog. But I stopped doing that because it was a hassle to edit and cut up the photos, and also it's not so pretty."

In what way do you think your age influences your blogging and do you ever get annoyed by the constant focus on your age?
"I used to get annoyed by the age comments but at least they're saying something, right? If readers are awed by my age, then they can go ahead. It's flattering, but I really don't see what the big deal is. I just concentrate on the blog, on what I think is cool, and try not to worry about the comments."

How do your parents feel about your blog?
"My entire family is insanely supportive of my blog. It's fun for them and they get to stay up-to-date on my activities and my state of mind. I'm very lucky that they like it, imagine if they didn't! I definitely wouldn't be where I am now."

What is the most remarkable thing that has happened since you started blogging?
"WHOWHATWEAR.COM contacted me to model in an editorial for them;

BLOG TITLE
The Stylish Wanderer

URL
www.thestylishwanderer.com

EDITOR
-

YEAR OF BIRTH
1995

ONLINE SINCE
2008

COUNTRY
USA

LANGUAGE
English

POSTS PER WEEK
3

VISITORS PER DAY
2500

TAGS
runway, photography, personal style

FAVOURITE BLOGS
www. lisaplace.devote.se
+
www.knighttcat.com
+
www.fashionsquad.com
+
www.luluandyourmom.blogspot.com
+
www.karlascloset.blogspot.com

by Elina Tozzi

TEEN VOGUE and AMERICAN APPAREL have contacted me for various things. I'm also the columnist for the TEEN UGLY section of CHICTOPIA. COM. These are all small steps leading to something big, though I can't yet imagine what."

What kind of reader do you envision when you are writing your blog?
"I guess I kind of imagine a girl about sixteen or seventeen that likes to have fun and be inspired by beautiful images. However, my terrific followers that comment seem older. Truthfully, I don't really think about it all that much, but I definitely can't imagine guys reading my blog! I mean, I know of a few guy bloggers who read it, but I certainly don't envision the male species when writing and putting my pictures up."

Are you in touch with other bloggers?
"Of course! I've had several blogger meet-ups in real life, and we also twitter each other a lot. Because we all love the same things it's easy to relate with one another, so meeting up is also a lot of fun. Sometimes we go to the beach, or eat lunch or go shopping. It's like you're with your friends from school except they're from the blogging world. It's so awesome."

How would you describe your personal style?
"My style changes every day! I have no way to really define it in a few words. Blogging has helped me so much though, in the sense that I now know what I like and what fits my figure, what is flattering and what isn't. Blogging is the best way to find out more about yourself and your personal style."

Who are your style icons?
"Zooey Deschanel, for her whimsical vintage style, Mary-Kate Olsen, for being downright cool, the statue-esque beautiful Irina Lazareanu, Marion Cotillard, Audrey Hepburn for classic style and simplicity, and Cleopatra."

What are your future plans? Do you aspire to work in the fashion industry?
"Blogging is definitely helpful for breaking into the industry, but whether I want to do it or not? I'm not really sure right now. It seems like such a difficult business. But I bet I'll probably work in retail for an after-school job in High School. One thing I can guarantee is that I definitely want to go to New York or Paris for fashion week one year. That's one of my dreams, to actually see the garments flowing and moving in all their glory up on the runway. "

How do you see the future of fashion blogs?
"Fashion blogs are just going to get better and more outstanding, and I guarantee you that the editors of tomorrow's magazines will all be veteran bloggers."

GARBAGE DRESS

Zana Bayne is attracted to all things black and shiny, and consequently her favourite dresses often end up having the appearance of garbage bags. Her blog title was born. "Evocative of my aesthetic, yet still slightly anonymous without being silly." Miss GARBAGE DRESS takes the floor.

"I have been blogging on various websites since I was in middle school. In my last years of livejournaling, I was mainly posting on fashion communities, where other fashionistas like Camille of CHILDHOOD FLAMES and Misha of DUSTY DRESS were posting before they started their independent blogs. Initiating GARBAGE DRESS was kind of like a natural progression, and a complete regression at the same time. Right now, my content is mostly image-based, with small accompanying anecdotes."

The drama of dressing up
"I tend to go back and forth between two very different mentalities of dressing; minimalism and excess. I prefer to wear one colour at a time, but then play with shade, texture, and proportion. I like to wear dresses because they create an outfit using only one garment. Other times, I love the decadence and drama of dressing up without regard to appropriateness of occasion. If I were to describe my personal style in one word, I would say 'evolutionary'. Having a blog on which I constantly document what I wear gives me a nice challenge, to rethink how I can experiment within my existing wardrobe."

Mom likes DEMEULEMEESTER
"I am inspired by happenstance inspirations, instead of specific celebrities. However, my mother will always be someone who I look up to for many reasons, one of them being her incredible sense of style. Mom likes DEMEULEMEESTER, okay?"

Zana Bayne vs. thin, tanned, blond bloggers with pretty make-up
"Wait, are you saying that I don't have pretty make-up? That aside, I think that I represent 'living proof' of an alternative to all of the qualities you mentioned above. But I'm going to have to also stick up and say that one of my best girls in San Francisco is thin, tan, with long blond hair and the prettiest make-up. She is a phenomenal dresser and I love her to death. I've never been a believer that your genetic makeup is the final determinant of your ability to look presentable. That part is up to you."

BLOG TITLE
Garbage Dress

URL
www.garbagedress.com

EDITOR
Zana Bayne

YEAR OF BIRTH
1988

ONLINE SINCE
2008

COUNTRY
USA/ Germany/ elsewhere

LANGUAGE
English

POSTS PER WEEK
7-14

VISITORS PER DAY
-

TAGS
black, shiny, serious-fun

FAVOURITE BLOGS
www.thefoxyman.blogspot.com
+
www.jakandjil.com
+
www.sixsixsick.blogspot.com
+
www.skelemitz.wordpress.com
+
www.gothsinhotweather.com

by Kirstin Hanssen

Reader profile

"I really blog as if I were writing to myself. I've had responses from fifteen-year-old boys, and comments from my mother. I am constantly surprised and overjoyed to learn the identity of my readers, whether they are complete strangers or people who I already have some sort of connection to in my present life."

Fashionable roommate

"I have been reading Katja's blog GLAMCANYON for a couple of years now, from her New York days, to London, to Berlin. When I announced on my blog last summer that I would be travelling through London, her and I met for the first time. She seemed to be running in the same sort of circles that I did, just in different cities. We actually ended up sharing a flat during my three months in Berlin, but I don't think that I was the best roommate. I'm bad at cleaning…"

Fashion blogs vs. fashion mags

"I think that whoever provides the best content will stay on top. Although there are many blogs that I click through daily, I own magazines that I will keep re-reading for years to come. Time is a factor that really differentiates the two; a magazine has months to research, plan, and devise content, while bloggers must churn out posts daily to stay relevant. With this time-collapse, it is hard to maintain a high level of inspiring, creative, well-presented imagery and text. Especially since blog-time also competes with job-time, life-time, and any other sort of normality. There is a reason why many of us will spend ridiculous amounts of money on paper publications. Would you spend $24 every three months to read my blog?"

ALICE POINT

Alicja Zielasko is the quirky and style-savvy blonde behind Polish blog ALICE POINT. Hailing from the historic city of Krakow, to say Alicja did not grow up in a booming fashion capital is a bit of an understatement. But, she explains to us, fashion blogging is very much alive in Poland, so much so that there is even a word for *fashion blogger* in Polish. Furthermore, featuring translations into English of her posts also allows Alicja's readers from far beyond the Polish border to join in the fun, and not without effect: ALICE POINT is included in the list of daily must-reads of the biggest fashion bloggers in the world.

Why did you start your blog and what is it about?
"First of all, I was fascinated by Scandinavian blogs. I thought, why not try it myself? I wanted to prove that Polish girls are stylish and imaginative too. My blog is mostly about fashion and a little bit about my life. I want to share my ideas and passion with other people around the world."

Why did you choose the name ALICE POINT?
"Alice is my real name. I added 'Point' to make the name sound more like a place on the internet. ALICE POINT - my point of view on fashion, trends, and style."

What is the most remarkable thing that has happened since you started blogging?
"A portrait of me made by Danny Roberts. It was a very nice surprise for me."

When we think of fashion, Poland isn't the first country that comes to mind, what do we need to know that we don't know yet?
"Fashion in Poland has changed and developed greatly in recent years. Poles follow the latest trends and want to be kept up-to-date with fashion. We have almost all of the clothing chain stores here. We have talented fashion designers, and there are more and more fashion shows and events in Poland. There is one thing that we're still missing, though: a Polish edition of VOGUE."

How is the blogging scene in Poland?
"The blogging scene is really big in Poland. We have over 200 blogs and the number is still growing – it shows that more and more people in

BLOG TITLE
Alice Point

URL
www.alicepoint.blogspot.com

EDITOR
Alicja Zielasko

YEAR OF BIRTH
1988

ONLINE SINCE
April 2008

COUNTRY
Poland

LANGUAGE
Polish/ English

POSTS PER WEEK
2

VISITORS PER DAY
3000

TAGS
outfits, style, trends

FAVOURITE BLOGS
www.elenita.no
+
www.fashiontoast.com
+
www.karlascloset.blogspot.com
+
www.modetrumman.se/
myblomquist

by Elina Tozzi

Poland are interested in fashion and want to share their passion with other people. We even have a special Polish name for fashion blogger: *Szafiarka*, which derives from the Polish word for wardrobe."

Do you think fashion blogs are more interesting and inspiring than fashion magazines?
"For me that's right. I find a lot of inspiration in the blogosphere: I can see real fashion from the street that is not as expensive as that in fashion magazines."

What are your future plans? Do you aspire to work in the fashion industry, and do you think your blog is a step-up to that?
"Yes, I want to work in fashion and I hope my blog will help me achieve that. I would like to be a stylist, a fashion journalist, or to cooperate with a clothing company. Maybe I will design clothes... Time will tell."

CREATURES
OF THE NIGHT

CREATURES OF THE NIGHT

Scenesters are on a constant chase for the next great thing; they are not afraid to rule the streets with fierceness and extravagance. They take inspiration from those who aren't restricted by rules, those who question boundaries, and they apply it to their own lives. It makes them look different and original, as fashion is a reflection of personal vision. It is these scenesters that shape modern culture. They are curious, independent, and aren't - as opposed to fashion designers or musicians - limited by commercial pressures.

History has known many scenesters. We saw them strutting themselves to death in the movie PARTY MONSTER, and voguing as if their lives depended on it in the documentary PARIS IS BURNING. In the early eighties, they ruled the streets of London under the name of 'New Romantics', a movement that continues to influence music, fashion, and arts in the UK. Contrary to today's scenesters, the New Romantics were relatively unknown, and didn't have the opportunity to show off their style, attitude and opinions to the entire world. The internet grants people the power to do exactly that. Naturally, an extravagant, somewhat narcissistic scenester would want to show the world who they are. They know exactly what they are doing, because influential (fashion) blogs have the power to do what traditional media, such as newspapers and fashion magazines, cannot. Due to the democratic qualities of the medium, any outspoken personality can transform into a superstar by just the number of hits on their blog or image.

With that knowledge a new breed of scenesters has risen. They are aware of their originality and are - sometimes all too - conscious of what an extraordinary photograph can lead to. And however clever that may be, this also can come across as forced, milking their looks like a one trick pony. The danger for today's scenesters lies in becoming some sort of marketing product: the outcome of a generation raised in an advertisement-driven society.

It's a hell of a task, relentlessly advertising your personal promotional campaign, everywhere you go. After all, 'avant-garde' is the scenester's middle name, so the stars of today could be gone by tomorrow. It thus becomes a necessity to be on top of your game constantly. In a society that tends to become shallower by the day, it is no wonder the limelight can be too bright for some. Scenesters aren't products or image builders of their own persona. They are human beings - something they themselves tend to forget.

So where to go when the spotlight literally blinds you and has you running for a breath of fresh air? You'll find scenesters in that same position on the internet, the place crowded with images of you rocking the most marvellous outfits. There are forums and communities to share opinions and feelings from the safe haven of your computer, the place where you can be fab in just your pyjamas. There, at night, when you give yourself some peace of mind and enjoy the wonderful looks fellow scenesters have created, is when the posing stops. A true scenester can be outlandish without any sort of fashion armour.

Through communities and blogs, today's youngsters unite in a world where individuality rules. And by doing that, their scene is more global and visible than ever before. The world offers the opportunity to learn from those who dare to stand out and

by Aynouk Tan

experiment. Anyone can copy and paste pictures so that they, too, are inspired to celebrate anarchy and freedom of mind. While doing that, please remember to stop and pose when a camera is nearby: be ready for the limelight to shine upon you! 'Cause a true 21st century scenester is always aware of where that picture could lead them.

ABOUT
Aynouk Tan

Aynouk Tan is fashion editor, art director, and 'scenester extraordinaire'. She writes a weekly column in the prestigious Dutch newspaper NRC HANDELS-BLAD. Besides that, she works for fashion magazines such as ZOO and L'OFFICIEL, builds art installations, and poses willingly for all cameras, rather like AB FAB's Patsy Stone. She parades all under the well-considered creed: "Fashion is party, let's celebrate!"

www.aynouktan.com

FAVOURITE BLOGS
www.fantasticman.com
+
(Bill Cunningham / via NYT)
www.nytimes.com/pages/
fashion
+
www.krautboys.blogspot.com
+
www.dennisduijnhouwer.com

GLAMCANYON

Katja Hentschel is the driving force behind GLAMCANYON. Before she turned it into a blog, GLAMCANYON was a website with just party photos. After joining a photography competition in New York, Katja decided to mix the party shots with street fashion pictures, and her blog was born. "I do still prefer party photos," Katja tells us, "they excite me. I see mine as little pieces of art. Street fashion is an amazing testimony of our time, but artistically less interesting to me."

Today Katja works as a professional photographer. "Most of my income is in one way or another connected to my success with GLAMCANYON, but I also shoot fashion, music portraits, and other stuff that is not related to it. I'm sure that without my blog I wouldn't be able to live off photography," she explains. Katja checks her blog for about ten minutes each day and needs another fifteen to post her pics. With the rising numbers in readership came attention from international media. "I was lucky enough to get noticed by magazines, newspapers, and TV programmes reporting on GLAMCANYON. I hope my blog is not too mainstream despite this attention. But I think GLAMCANYON-viewers are a particular lot. In a good way. "

Do you think you inspire other people or set trends with your blog?
"I wouldn't say I set trends with my blog, but I get a chance to show what's worth showing. People tell me that the fashion styles in the photos inspire them, which I think is great. I love getting inspiration from other people's work, so to be able to do that for someone else in return is wonderful."

How would you describe your personal style, and does blogging influence the way you dress?
"A good chunk of my wardrobe is vintage and if you check GLAMCANYON you'll notice that most of the people I photograph wear vintage too. That's my personal stamp on the blog. Style blogging influences me at times when I see an outfit I really like and then catch myself looking for something similar in the shops."

Do you feel you have become an authority in representing the 'hipster community'?
"I don't think I am any type of authority of any community. I just want to

BLOG TITLE
Glamcanyon

URL
www.glamcanyon.blogspot.com

EDITOR
Katja Hentschel

YEAR OF BIRTH
1982

ONLINE SINCE
May 2007

COUNTRY
UK

NATIONALITY
German

LANGUAGE
English

POSTS PER WEEK
6

VISITORS PER DAY
1100-2000

TAGS
colourful, cool, edgy

FAVOURITE BLOGS
www.styleslut.blogspot.com
+
www.thesartorialist.blogspot.com
+
www.lesmads.de

by Kirstin Hanssen

do my thing and if a few people look at my stuff and think 'cool',
then I have achieved all I wanted to achieve."

How would you explain the success of street style blogs?
"I think it's a mix of *Schaulust*, a certain curiosity to see what other
people are wearing and the hunt for inspiration and trends. I do think
that street style blogs are shaping fashion to a good degree nowadays."

Are you in touch with other bloggers?
"Yeah, I do know quite a few by now. We meet at certain events and we
all get along pretty well. I can say that all successful bloggers I have met
are very interesting, versatile, and have strong personalities. They've
essentially crafted their own career based on a blog, so you have got
to respect that."

What is the street style in Berlin like?
"Berlin is all about comfort. People enjoy fashion and many are buying
from young designers, but the big thing is to wear something that is both
original and comfortable. So lots of oversized pieces and plain colours.
When you look at the work of Berlin designer labels such as REALITY
STUDIO, JULIAANDBEN, WOLFEN, or WUNDERKIND you will know what
I mean."

What is the most remarkable thing that has happened since you started blogging?
"Well, turning pro as a photographer was a massive step considering that I was actually training to become a psychologist. I now run columns in two big German publications, my clients include NOKIA, ABSOLUT, SONY, and COCA COLA, and recently I directed my first music video. I can definitely see myself doing more of that."

How do you see the future of your blog and of fashion blogs in general?
"I have no clue, but I think it's smart to start a blog, as it's the best way to show off your talent and ambition to the nation It will almost certainly help you get a job in the fashion/publishing industry."

SHARK VS. BEAR

With partypic blogs as our witness, we may be tempted to believe that New York, Los Angeles, and Paris are where the action is. But Kavin Wong of SHARK VS. BEAR proves that Toronto can hold its ground. Frustrated by the impersonal and robotic approach of party photographers in the local club scene, he decided in early 2007: "Oh, I can do better than that!" So Wong started his own photo blog, and picked the most nonsensical name he could think of as its title. We asked Wong all about his experiences over the last two years and he told us about his obsession with taking photos and a certain bathroom incident...

What sets SHARK VS. BEAR apart from other party photo blogs?

"There are other party photo sites? Damn. It's different because every person with a camera takes pictures differently and because it has different people in our different city. It's the same because it features mostly young people, where most of them are having a good time, listening to similar music, wearing similar clothes, reading similar fashion blogs. In terms of photos, I try to capture the boisterous moment of everyone having a good time. Most of the time, everyone looks good, and in the off chance they don't, at least they sure look like they are enjoying themselves."

What are your criteria for selecting locations and events to visit?

"I decide based on how much fun the event will be for me, and for other people. The goal is to take interesting pictures, and if the event only has five awkward teenagers with bad teeth, it may not be...oh wait, that actually sounds like a good party!"

What is specific about the party and fashion scene in Toronto?

"There's a large supportive community. Toronto has a lot of music talent and has recently been getting international recognition. And since party culture is heavily tied in with music, we are always looking out for each other. 'So and so is playing at this and that, let's go!' We don't have much of a fashion style, but we make it up for being outgoing."

What is the most remarkable, shocking, juicy thing that has happened since you started blogging?

"I had my camera smashed to the ground and flushed in the toilet. That was the only real violence I witnessed. The camera was completely

BLOG TITLE
Shark vs. Bear

URL
www.sharkvsbear.com

EDITOR
Kavin Wong

YEAR OF BIRTH
-

ONLINE SINCE
March 2007

COUNTRY
Canada

LANGUAGE
English

POSTS PER WEEK
1

VISITORS PER DAY
500

TAGS
photography, party, colourful

FAVOURITE BLOGS
-

by Elina Tozzi

destroyed, but I wasn't hurt. And as an example of the loving community in Toronto, there was a charity event the very next week by local promoters and artists to help raise money for a new camera for me!"

Do you have groupies?
"I have friends who I met from going out so frequently, and sometimes we have brunch together."

How has being a party photographer influenced your way of partying and dressing?
"I don't party unless I have a camera now. It may sound like a drag, but it's not because I am having so much fun doing it. We can compare it to the association of alcohol and cigarettes with partying. For a lot of people, you go out and you drink and smoke. For me, I go out and drink and take pictures. I also reached a point where I have a pathological replacement of memories and moments with a photograph. Did it really happen if no one photographed it? In terms of fashion style, it made me lazier. I don't even try anymore. I just buy a three-pack of T-shirts for $9.99, and have been rocking the same pair of LEVI'S I had for two years."

As a cultural phenomenon, what do you think blogs and party photo websites tell us about our time?
"We are obsessed with celebrities and being famous. But is this anything new? Self-publication is very popular, and it provides an outlet for anybody to be broadcast. However, you will have to produce something of quality if you want your audience to reach beyond your circle of family and friends. Not all blogs are vehicles to promote oneself, they also serve as a medium that encourages the individual to practice their craft periodically. To create and get feedback, to share. Initially, I wanted to separate my identity from the site. I didn't want to include pictures of myself, or have my name attached to it. But eventually, the site became more personal and now it's about having fun with my friends."

Can you make a living through your blog?
"The site doesn't make money, but there are great rewards. I did try asking GOOGLE for money, but they thought the site has 'Adult Content'. And when I went to the good banner affiliates, it turned out I didn't drive enough traffic. So I'm in the middle ground, which is how I like to keep it. Now I don't depend on the site for rent money and I can post when and what I want."

What do you hope to achieve with SHARK VS. BEAR and what are your plans for the future?
"I got laid a few times. I also learned a lot because of going out and taking so many photos. I know how to use some of these knobs on top of the camera, and am more comfortable telling people what to do. My future plan is to continue learning, which may or may not include a website."

THE COBRA SNAKE

Mark Hunter lives the life of a rock star. This becomes all the more apparent when we enter his Amsterdam hotel room on a Wednesday morning in February 2009. Clothes and promotional items are scattered across the floor. Having spent the evening before at a Ladyhawke performance, Hunter and Steve Aoki - DJ and partner in crime - just dragged themselves out of bed, and indeed look like they've been up all night. Hunter clearly struggles to concentrate on the questions we fire away at him, while Aoki keeps clicking away on his laptop. When a fan comes by to pick out a genuine COBRA SNAKE T-shirt, both veer their full attention at the young man, who later leaves with not only the shirt but also autographs of the pair, and is smiling from ear to ear. Later, as the interview comes to a close, Hunter and Aoki most casually inform us they have a plane to catch — in a mere thirty minutes. Just another day at the office for pop culture icons.

Hunter started photographing the young and good-looking at parties in his hometown of L.A. in 2004, posting the photos on his blog POLAROID SCENE. Within a matter of two years, Hunter, now using the alter ego THE COBRA SNAKE, had become one of the main faces of 'hipster culture', and the forerunner of the fashion blogging phenomenon. In 2006, his blog featured a then-unknown Cory Kennedy, propelling her to stardom at the age of sixteen. Kennedy, who was Mark's girlfriend at the time, became one of the very first internet celebrities due to her appearance on Hunter's blog.

What does the name THE COBRA SNAKE represent?
"It's endless, the name is endless and meaningless, so it's going to turn out to much more than just photos. You know, it's not even just about me, it's about a much larger idea. The name won't limit me. Other websites directly reference parties and nightlife, and I'm here to do so much more than nightlife and parties: there are photos of the daytime, at the beach, there are photos of fashion week, of art shows… I also shoot for magazines and stuff a lot, but those photos I don't really put on the website."

How do you select locations or events to visit? What are your criteria?
"I basically just travel the world, usually with my friend Steve, he's a world-famous DJ, and we go around wherever promoters want him to perform, most of the time it's very young, emerging fashionable

BLOG TITLE
The Cobra Snake

URL
www.thecobrasnake.com

EDITOR
Mark Hunter

YEAR OF BIRTH
1985

ONLINE SINCE
2003

COUNTRY
USA

LANGUAGE
English

POSTS
daily

VISITORS PER DAY
25000

TAGS
-

FAVOURITE BLOGS
www.coolcats.fr
+
www.colette.fr
+
www.hipsterrunoff.com
+
www.theselby.com
+
www.dimmak.com

by Elina Tozzi & Kirstin Hanssen

countries and markets. This time we're going all over Europe, but we've been to Australia, we've been to pretty much anywhere you could imagine. And then, you know, I'm super passionate about fashion, so I go to Paris fashion week and New York fashion week and I went to Brazil for fashion week. I try to mix it up to give the best sort of photos to the website."

How do you select your models and subjects?
"Mostly at parties, so I just look for people that look interesting, they're dressed well, and then I photograph them. What's good style? I think good style is when you're unique and different. There's something special to each person, so you can be fat, you can be short, you can be super skinny, you can be anything, and if you can dress in a way that suits you and complements your features... It's about discovering what looks good on you."

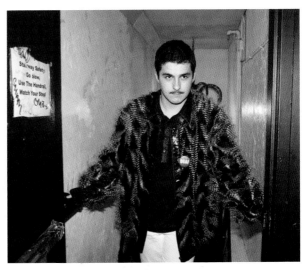

How do people respond to you when you are taking photos?
"Yeah I'm very hairy, so people recognise me. And yeah, it's crazy to have a following internationally pretty much everywhere I go, I think it helps when people know me and I'm taking pictures of like really pretty girls or cool-looking people because it makes them understand it better, when I say oh it's for THE COBRA SNAKE, otherwise they think I'm weird or something, haha."

Do you ever notice people trying to grab your attention, simply because they want their picture to be on the internet?
"I don't really pay attention to that..."

Party photos sometimes go pretty far, in terms of showing alcohol abuse, nudity, and even violence. What do you consider to be too much or too graphic?
"I try to keep it PG13, like in the movie ratings. If there was violence, I would prefer to help the situation, or try to at least, than make it worse, and I'm not a big fan of nudity or... whatever else you said, drug-use."

For instance, do girls voluntarily take their clothes off?
"No. I don't really promote that. Keep your clothes on, haha!"

As a cultural phenomenon, what do you think blogs and party photo websites tell us about our time?
"Blogging is really cool. It's a really good way to present yourself and your ideas on the internet on such a large scale, you can really make a big impact with very little money, very little energy. You can type something and a million people can read it, you can take a picture and everyone in the world can see it, so it's really exciting, that's what has made me so successful. I travel a lot, so it makes sense that the website has such a wide recognition everywhere, but without travelling the internet can still spread you to every country in the world."

How do you think people in fifty or a hundred years will look at the phenomenon of blogging?

"Well, I think it's getting more and more relevant, blogs are better than magazines now. More people are paying attention to what STYLE.COM is saying than what happens in VOGUE next month, so I think it's only going to become more of a credible thing."

You have a web shop with T-shirts and also vintage clothing on THE COBRA SNAKE. Can you tell us more about this business and what we can expect from it in the future?

"Everyone is always emailing me, asking 'where did you get those clothes' and 'where did that girl get her shoes', or 'where did you find that T-shirt', and slowly I'm trying to be able to turn that into a shop, where I can answer those questions. I'm super into finding really unique things when I travel, and sometimes they don't fit me, so then I can sell them to other people they might be better for."

What are your future plans?

"Well, I'd rather just do them and not talk about them, because then people say 'oh you never did that', and 'he talks too much'! But I think that everybody can be independently successful and try to do something different. If you're passionate about being an artist, do it, if you want to make music, make music, if you want to do fashion design, start making clothes! There are no limits anymore."

PRETEND IT NEVER HAPPENED

Colourful and outrageous party people dominate the photos on PRETEND IT NEVER HAPPENED. The blog was born on a late night in bed when Joost Vandebrug came up with an idea. He wanted to start a blog featuring party shots he and his pal Clyde Burrows were making in cities like Amsterdam, London, Antwerp, Paris, and Madrid. "The name refers to the feeling many might have experienced waking up after a wild party and remembering some embarrassing behaviour," says Clyde, explaining the perfectly fitting title for the platform he and Joost are currently building.

Besides the blog, the duo organises parties under the same name, and are also working on a new website with additional features, music, photos, fashion, and contributors. When asked what he hopes to achieve with PRETEND IT NEVER HAPPENED Clyde answers: "world fame of course!" But immediately, and much more modestly, he adds: "Just joking... it would be nice to show the little boys and girls who feel different and are stuck in a small country village that there is a whole different world out there. They are not alone! We want to show them places where they can fit in, and I hope our blog inspires them to keep expressing themselves."

Dress like TV stars

Party or nightlife photography can often be considered to document a specific scene, but Clyde doesn't particularly like that term. "Some of my friends speak of scenes too often," he explains. "I just like to go to parties with people who understand how to dress nice as it makes it more fun to watch them. I'm not good at giving people a special group name." The cultural phenomenon of blogging and party photo websites can, in Clyde's view, best be compared to that of television in the past. "For a long time people were inspired by TV. They wanted to dress like TV stars, eat like them, etc. Now, we have so-called internet celebs. People just want someone to look up to!"

This 'new thing' called blogging

PRETEND IT NEVER HAPPENED regularly features a group of young Dutch kids that are currently on the fast track to becoming the new faces in Dutch fashion, due to their appearance in magazines and on the world's biggest fashion blogs. "Yes, they are special. They are all very talented,

BLOG TITLE
Pretend It Never Happened

URL
www.pretenditneverhappened.
blogspot.com

EDITORS
Clyde Burrows,
Joost Vandebrug

YEAR OF BIRTH
1989, 1982

ONLINE SINCE
November 2008

COUNTRY
The Netherlands

LANGUAGE
English

POSTS PER WEEK
"depends on the good parties"

VISITORS PER DAY
min. 600

TAGS
parties, people

FAVOURITE BLOGS
www.katelovesme.net
+
www.sachahilton.blogspot.com
+
www.buvezmadison.blogspot.com

by Kirstin Hanssen

look and dress amazing, and have big dreams. It's their youth and enthusiasm that attracts people I believe, but also the fact that they don't
fit in with the masses, especially not in the Dutch mainstream." This is
probably also why the Dutch fashion blogging culture is lagging behind
on what is happening across the borders. "Well, there may be more
reasons for that, but the most important one is that Dutch people don't
really dress that extraordinary. It often occurs that people on the street
start yelling or staring at my friends and me, whereas in London, Paris
or New York, people don't seem to be surprised by our appearance.
So, yes, the average Dutchman isn't exactly a style pioneer, and I think
most people here have no clue about the phenomenon of fashion blogging thus far."

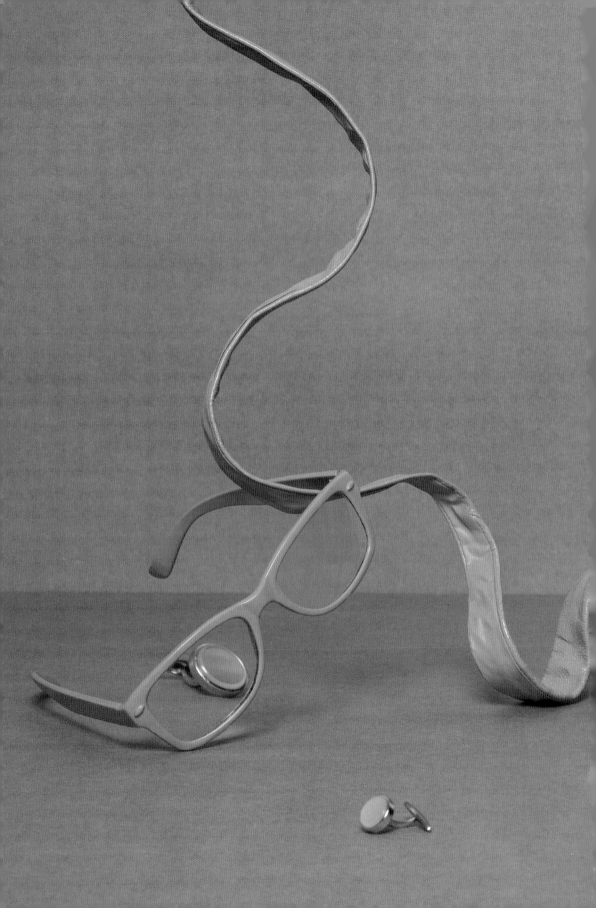

WHAT ABOUT THE BOYS?

WHAT ABOUT THE BOYS?

Today, blogs are an excellent medium for industry geeks wanting to stay up-to-date. A large portion of the - mainly internationally oriented - fashion blogs are devoted to young and unknown labels, in addition to general updates on established designers and the fashion weeks. For the guys there are even specialised men's blogs that primarily report on the attire of the fashion-conscious man. Archive magazine images often dominate the scroll pages of these blogs, interjected by photos of the blogger in every conceivable pose and outfit.

Exhibitionism isn't uncommon on the blogs of 'young writers and writerettes', and in them we can distinguish a specific fascination for dressing in a determined and contemporary fashion. Posing in a set by yet undiscovered designers, or in a styling mix of well-established labels, allows the blog visitor to feel inspired. These images do not affect my personal wardrobe, but that is mainly due to my unwavering style and taste.

Photos and videos of the latest shows in Paris, London, Milan, and NY aren't a source of inspiration for me either. However, global underground reports are; with their backstage photography of happenings a passionate fashion lover can't always attend. And indeed, as a fashion victim in this multidisciplinary age, it is nearly inconceivable not to explore the visual arts, architecture, and design (all of which are increasingly visible on blogs) as well. Quite a bit, then, is demanded of bloggers... You would have to be a true fashion addict to be part of five different scenes at a time, soaking up impressions from one event after another. But: you certainly get something in return! In the past seasons, bloggers have been seated front row at fashion shows and treated as VIP's at openings.

They are now considered part of a truly legitimate medium.

As a regular visitor of blogs, you imagine yourself backstage at shows and events you might never be able to attend physically. And, as a bonus, there's a snapshot of the designer, posing with the blogger, new BFF's it might seem, in front of a rack of his or her latest creations. For a talent scout like myself, there is great value in being able to see the person behind the work!

The diversity within the fashion blogosphere is abound; there is something there for everyone. For the critics among us, I have one piece of advice: this 'street journalism' is unstoppable, and resisting is pointless. My device is: surrender yourself to it, find out what suits you, consider yourself enriched, and enjoy! Personally, I tend to avoid most fashion blogs out there, and yet the interesting ones absorb me and immerse me into a world of passion and boundless opportunities.

The last crucial point of interest revolves around the question of whether bloggers can be considered to be professional autodidacts, or whether blogs merely provide easy-to-consume info and impressions. In any case, blogs have proven to be a new digital PR channel, allowing extraordinarily quick and easy international spread of news. One remarkable symptom is that blogs are increasingly sponsored via companies' PR budgets. Whether that affects the blog's objectivity is a question worth asking. Indeed, it is the lack of commercial interest that creates a platform for objectivity, and this is precisely what sets blogs apart. So, will the disappearance of the underground and the possible decrease of objectivity sustain the

by Carlo Wijnands

blogosphere or not? Or will we soon distinguish two separate blog concepts: the personal vision and the magazine-like vision?

One thing is certain: blogs are taking over a large portion of magazines' 'fast' informational value, hence placing the two in direct competition. Magazines will be forced to go back to their roots as expert medium, featuring in-depth interviews, background stories, trends and developments. To me this would seem like a very pleasant division of roles for the future.

ABOUT
Carlo Wijnands

Being the talent scout of HTNK fashion recruitment & consultancy, Carlo Wijnands is constantly on the lookout for new and inspiring fashion designer signatures. Wijnands lectures at various fashion academies and is involved in several advisory boards and selection committees of fashion-related platforms and events.

www.htnk.nl

FAVOURITE BLOGS
www.stylesalvage.blogspot.com
+
www.ashadedviewonfashion.com
+
www.tavi-thenewgirlintown.blogspot.com
+
www.stylebubble.co.uk
+
(Milou van Rossum, Volkskrant)
www.vkblog.nl/blog/6606/mode
+
www.fashiontoast.com
+
www.katelovesme.net

STYLE SALVAGE

Whilst at Warwick University, best friends Steve Salter and EJ (a.k.a. Eliza – who doesn't like to give much away on her persona) would make a dash for the clothing shops whenever their student loan came in. During that time, their ongoing 'chinwag' on style and fashion bloomed, and grew out to become one of the first and arguably the finest online guide on contemporary menswear today.

Taking just a glimpse at STYLE SALVAGE, one couldn't imagine that the two-force army behind the blog has a day job, one that is totally unrelated to the fashion industry. Steve works at a digital network, and EJ's profession "is completely irrelevant, for the blog at least." Steve says: "While I was working in London and EJ in Manchester, we spent far too much of our time sending each other procrastinating emails, containing everything from bargain finds to high street releases, Fred Astaire's style tips to Stockholm street style snaps. The dialogue around men's style has always been there for us and one day, we just thought 'Why not make a blog together?' and so we did!"

How did STYLE SALVAGE evolve?
"When we started blogging back in 2007, there were very few blogs dedicated to men's style, but thankfully over the past few years more and more are being launched. We wanted the blog to be a discussion, not just between the two of us, but to hear from the readers as well. As the blog evolved we've been able to interview people working in the industry that we really admire. We never imagined that we'd interview peoples like FANTASTIC MAN's Charlie Porter, the B STORE chaps and certainly not some of our favourite designers including CAROLYN MASSEY, MR. HARE, CASELY-HAYFORD, and Patrick Grant of NORTON & SONS, and E. TAUTZ."

What role does blogging occupy in your daily life?
Steve: "Blogging is an addictive pastime and it's interwoven with my life. I do feel a need to post daily now. However, we always strive to seek out and write interesting posts, as opposed to just put something up to fill an imaginary quota. There is a tendency within the men's fashion blogosphere to write similar content to one another, and to be honest that has made us try even harder."

BLOG TITLE
Style Salvage

URL
www.stylesalvage.blogspot.com

EDITORS
Steve Salter, EJ

YEAR OF BIRTH
1984

ONLINE SINCE
June 2007

COUNTRY
UK

LANGUAGE
English

POSTS PER WEEK
5-8

VISITORS PER DAY
"It keeps on growing"

TAGS
men's fashion, men's style

FAVOURITE BLOGS
www.thedandyproject.blogspot.com
+
www.streetetiquette.com
+
www.wecouldgrowuptogether.blogspot.com
+
www.mrhares.blogspot.com
+
www.businessoffashion.com

by Kirstin Hanssen

EJ: "I generally have an eye out for things that inspire me. People watching, and particularly outfit watching is one of my favourite hobbies. I suppose this filters down to the blog."

What is the most remarkable thing that has happened since you started blogging?

Steve: "Sitting front row at a number of shows at London Fashion Week, and I'm also constantly surprised to hear that people that I really admire read the blog."

You clearly state "This is an ad-free blog". What is the reason for this?

"Over the last year or so, more and more brands and stores are approaching us, but it has always been our explicit intention to remain an ad-free blog. We feel that it could all get a little grey and complicated if you start putting ads up or accepting text links and advertorials. Ultimately, the blog is just a bit of fun for us."

How important are comments to you? And how you deal with the negative ones?

"It feels great to have people comment on one of our posts, and over the years we have amassed a number of different perspectives from regular readers. Fortunately, we don't receive too many negative comments, certainly not personal ones directed at the two of us. If someone does not like one of the designers or pieces we feature, then we welcome their opinion as long as they don't attack them for

ridiculous reasons. We have to delete spam comments far more often than unacceptable negative comments."

How do you think the growing influence of blogging alters the role of fashion magazines?

Steve: "With the rise of blogs, fashion news and information on the latest product releases in particular are old by the time even a weekly magazine is published. I still consume magazines in much the same way as I always have done, but I'd like to see them push it a bit more. I still look forward to getting my hands on the latest issue of FANTASTIC MAN every six months, but I think I've lost that feeling with most other publications. I think we will see magazines continuing to evolve from the throwaway monthly model we have all seen to much more limited and special releases, issues that we will cherish for years as opposed to minutes!"

What would be your dream come true, in terms of blogging?

Steve: "We don't have a fantasy with blogging. We aren't one of those blogs who wants to get into the industry through the back door. We blog because we enjoy it, and there isn't any more to it than that. Of course we love it when we get the opportunity to learn more about our favourite pieces and the designers and craftsmen who have made them, and I do hope this continues. My ultimate fantasy would be to open my own menswear store, and I hope to still be blogging when that happens one day in the distant future."

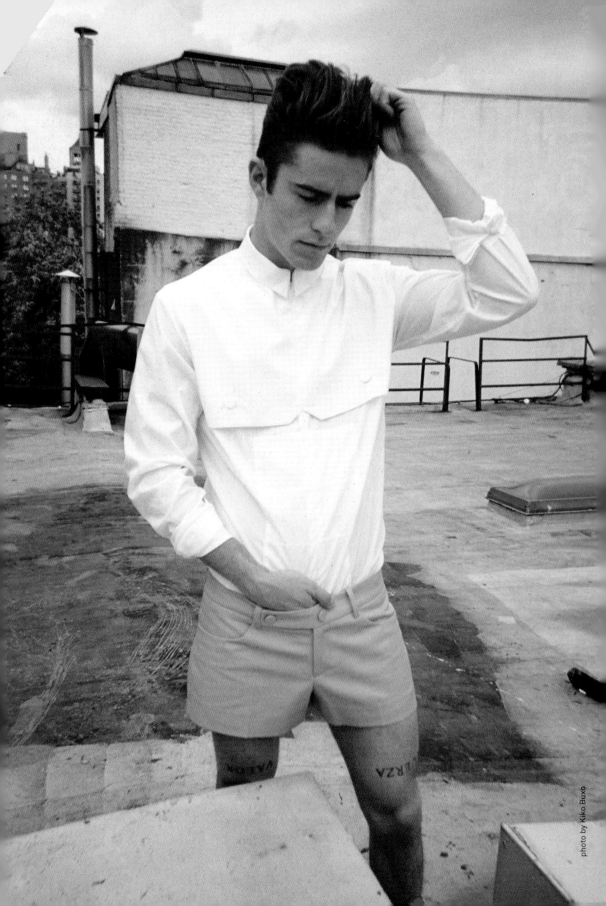

KATELOVESME

Central Saint Martins College of Art & Design student Pelayo Díaz Zapico knows how to rock a kilt. "I am a huge Kate Moss fan, but it was too evident to use that in my blog title. It would be nice if somehow she loved me back." Well, Kate probably does, because Pelayo, adored by both female and male lovers of the stylish and beautiful, is THE Adonis of fashion blogging.

"I was born in Oviedo, North Spain. Growing up in this small and beautiful but very traditional city was not really exciting, and so I moved away when I was only a teenager. I went to a religious school for about fourteen years. That really fucked me up, but at the same time I had so much fun there! After that, I studied at the School of Art in Oviedo, where I realised actually I could do stuff right. I worked in a shop, which I kept a secret from my dad, and saved some money to visit London for a weekend with my sister. I immediately loved the energy of the city and decided to be part of it. As soon as I finished high school I packed my brand new LOUIS VUITTON suitcase and flew away. The rest is history."

Why did you decide to start KATELOVESME?

"I need to tell a story, my story. Not only in a visual way, though I write less nowadays. I like to receive and read comments and somehow learn from it, though it's often more laughing than learning. My main focus is to keep a little diary on my opinions, parties, and inspirations. I mix stuff I take really seriously with stuff I couldn't care less about, confusing other people and sometimes even myself. A blog is an instrument to deal with others' opinions, without letting them influence you negatively. For me, every single one of us is amazing. No matter what someone else says."

What is the most remarkable thing that has happened since you started KATELOVESME?

"KATELOVESME has not really changed my life, in terms of visiting parties and wearing the clothes I do. I think that if I wouldn't run the blog, beautiful things would have come along my way anyhow. But from all the opportunities I got since people found me on my blog, like the fashion campaigns, the magazine editorials... the most remarkable thing is what happens every time someone stops me and tells me that he or she likes my blog, and that I should carry on. That gives me a great feeling."

BLOG TITLE
Katelovesme

URL
www.katelovesme.net

EDITOR
Pelayo Díaz Zapico

YEAR OF BIRTH
1986

ONLINE SINCE
2007

COUNTRY
UK

LANGUAGE
English / Spanish

POSTS PER WEEK
2

VISITORS PER DAY
5000

TAGS
authentic, fun, unpredictable

FAVOURITE BLOGS
www.amlul.com
+
www.hermanasmiranda.blogspot.com
+
www.margotbowman.blogspot.com

by Kirstin Hanssen

photos by (clockwise from top) Tamara Robles, Saga Sig, Gala G + Miranda M, & Saga Sig

Do you earn any money with KATELOVESME?
"I do. Not that I like talking about it."

Do you think you inspire other people?
"I guess anything you put up on the internet catches the eye of others, influencing them in one way or another. Sometimes I get emails from anonymous interns at fashion houses, just to let me know their boss put me up on their mood boards. I love that."

How did you create and evolve your unique personal style?
"I'm just myself; a mixture of the people I've met over the years, the places I've been, and things that have happened to me. I know it's the same answer all the time, but it really is the reason. We all become what we live."

You are close friends with another famous blogger, Gala Gonzalez…
"I met her in Barcelona at the VIP area of a famous club, back in 2005. She asked me about my T-shirt and I fell in love with her smile. We didn't speak or see each other for a year, until we met at Central Saint Martins. It took us about three months to realise we had already met. It was the greatest coincidence ever!"

What question do you get asked the most?
"A lot of, I guess, teenagers, ask me how I managed to become famous, as they want to do the same. Well, that's the problem… I'm probably successful because I don't want to follow in anyone's footsteps. But the most-asked question really is: 'How do you keep your hair like that?'"

How do you think the world of fashion blogs has changed in the past few years?
"It seems that everyone has a blog now, but not many people 'keep it real'. They create a character, just to grab attention. It's a pity, because it makes us look like we're all the same. Also, fashion blogs are full of people who don't really care about fashion, they are just obsessed, and that's sad."

What do you hope to achieve with your blog?
"The funny thing is I don't want to achieve anything. I'm not trying to win any awards here! I don't even like being called a 'blogger'. I blog because I enjoy doing it, putting my point across and keeping a record on things I do or am interested in. My generation is the first generation of bloggers, so we don't know where we are going or what's next. That's why I'm going to carry on; to find out and be able to answer that some day."

STREET ETIQUETTE

The Bronx-raised college students Joshua Kissi and Travis Gumbs are only twenty years of age, but that does not hinder them from dressing like gentlemen. The term 'contemporary dandyism' would probably match their spotless appearance best, since the handsome duo combines timeless classics with urban modernism, creating a new street vogue that inspires readers far beyond NYC. "STREET ETIQUETTE has changed our lives drastically, from being recognised on the street to carrying yourself in a certain light, because you are representing your 'brand' everywhere you go." A chat with Joshua.

Similar to the thousands who are just starting a blog, Joshua and Travis initially were indecisive on what kind of audience they wanted their site to cater to. "We went through months of just posting merchandise we thought were cool off sites like HYPEBEAST and SELECTISM. We still felt a void in what we were doing, knowing we wanted to do something more unique and standout. Possessing several characteristics that separated us from the rest, such as African-American, males, and Bronx-raised, we knew we had something up our sleeves. The blog really began to evolve when we started to post pictures of ourselves that correlated to what was being posted. With so many people on the same wavelength as us, individuals seemed to be starting to build a relationship with us simply via the internet. We receive many emails from readers we don't know, from various destinations, like France or Sweden, encouraging us to keep on with the site and telling us that we inspire them."

No income

"We have made the important and 'risky' decision of not incorporating ads on our site. Advertisements can be beneficial to a site depending on its direction, but we feel we can develop an actual relationship with the brand instead of just throwing up their ads to show support. We would rather schedule a meeting, sit down and come up with ideas on how we could benefit this brand using what we know and using STREET ETIQUETTE."

Male vs. female style bloggers

"Male style bloggers aren't as popular as our female counterparts, but there are a good amount of fantastic sites. I can say that it's still

BLOG TITLE
Street Etiquette

URL
www.streetetiquette.com

EDITORS
Joshua Kissi, Travis Gumbs

YEAR OF BIRTH
1989

ONLINE SINCE
June 2008

COUNTRY
USA

LANGUAGE
English

POSTS PER WEEK
1-2

VISITORS PER DAY
7000

TAGS
men's style , urban fashion

FAVOURITE BLOGS
www.jazzimcg.com/blog
+
www.seaofshoes.com
+
www.jakedavis.typepad.com
+
www.thestylishwanderer.blogspot.com
+
www.stylesalvage.blogspot.com

by Kirstin Hanssen – portrait photo by Rog Walker

a growing process in which many male style bloggers are slowly appearing. The days where you would be looked at as being feminine for spending time on how you dress and how you present yourself to the world are over."

Street style in The Bronx
"The Bronx street style pretty much doesn't exist when it comes to dressing in a way similar to what we do. It's a borough populated by over a million individuals. You can spot a few older gentlemen wearing what was popular in their day and age. The suit will never go out of style: it's a universal staple that someone who is serious about their image and business will take path to."

Comments
"Comments are very important to us, we strive to respond to every comment posted. It really improves the relationship between you and your readers, providing a more comfortable tangent. Since our blog caters more to the male perspective, we think there are typically more male comments being posted on our site. There is also a wide range of female readers checking our site who are inspired by what we do. It really works both ways."

FAQ
"The most-asked question that we receive has to be 'Where do you guys purchase your beads?' and the most remarkable has to be 'Are you guys single?'"

Growing influence of blogging
"The sky is the limit for fashion blogs, as they have taken on such an influential role in the few years they have been out. This influence is affecting the role of fashion magazines in such a significant way. The internet has now made information readily available, without having to run out to buy a physical magazine. When you do purchase a magazine, the information in it is aged compared to the up-to-date news you get on the internet. There is a shift in who provides valuable content, and internet fashion blogs are now running with it."

THE DANDY PROJECT

"Being dandy isn't as ancient or stuffy as you might think it to be," states Philippines-born Isidore Tuason, a.k.a. Izzy T., on his blog THE DANDY PROJECT. The advertising student - currently based in the US - has a knack for DIY-ing runway or designer items, especially those with a high 'quirk factor'. "I get inspired by the runway, street style blogs, or stylish people around me. When I see something with the DIY potential, I rush to the fabric or art supply store to buy the materials I need, and get on with the project while I'm high on inspiration."

What are your passions besides fashion?
"I love food: cooking, eating, and talking about it. I also practice Ashtanga yoga, and that keeps me calm and centred."

Why did you start THE DANDY PROJECT?
"I have so much to say about fashion, really strong opinions about sartorial matters, and I figured blogging would be the best medium for me to express these views. Since I started THE DANDY PROJECT, I gained a keener sense of my own personal style. Having photographs of my outfits put up on the internet for everybody to comment on helped me view my style more objectively."

When you first started the blog you sometimes made yourself unrecognisable in photos. Was that a conscious decision?
"I blurred my face out in my first few outfit posts because it took some time for me to get used to the fact that I was opening a part of my private life to the world through blogging. It may not be the same case for all, but for me, I eventually felt that I had to reveal more about myself in order to be taken more seriously and be considered an earnest voice in the fashion blogosphere."

Do you think your style is accepted in Manila? You picture yourself in a world of grey suits in your header graphic…
"I don't think it's a matter of being accepted or not, I think people in Manila are just generally amused with what I wear. I'm all about existentialism in fashion: no one should ever have the right to tell anyone what to wear and what not to wear."

BLOG TITLE
The Dandy Project

URL
www.thedandyproject.com

EDITOR
Isidore Tuason

YEAR OF BIRTH
1985

ONLINE SINCE
September 2008

COUNTRY
Philippines, currently USA

LANGUAGE
English

POSTS PER WEEK
1-4

VISITORS PER DAY
243

TAGS
dandy, personal style, fashion reviews

FAVOURITE BLOGS
www.stylesalvage.blogspot.com
+
www.robbiespencer.blogspot.com
+
www.dropsnap.jp
+
www.seaofshoes.com
+
www.thesartorialist.blogspot.com

by Kirstin Hanssen

How do you deal with negative comments?
"As long as the comments have the slightest hint of constructive criticism and aren't outright personal attacks, I publish them and try to learn as much from them as I can."

How would you describe 'dandyism'?
"I think there are so many types of dandies out there; dandy style melds well with other styles: hip-hop and street wear à la Kanye West, British punk, and surprisingly even with a darker, more enigmatic aesthetic as seen in ROBERT GELLER or ANN DEMEULEMEESTER. My own flavour of dandyism is open, experimental, and dressed-up."

Is your blog a way of connecting to like-minded dandies worldwide?
"I'm very grateful for how THE DANDY PROJECT helped me connect with people worldwide who share very specifically similar interests, not necessarily just dandies. Through my blog, I've gotten in touch with Joshua of STREET ETIQUETTE, Ca of THE CABLOG, and Frederic of TALES FROM FREDERIC, all of whom have their own brand of dandyism."

Men's fashion is a smaller industry compared to women's, does that make it easier to write about it?
"Yes, but at the same time, the smaller size of the industry makes it a challenge to find fresh material and to avoid falling into the trap of writing about something because there's nothing better to write about. That being said, I think there's a lot going on in men's fashion right now in terms of new designers in the most unexpected locations, and bloggers should lead the way in bringing these new creative minds in fashion into the public consciousness. In general, I'd say menswear excites me more because I enjoy seeing how creative minds in the industry concoct fashion that is fresh and outstanding, while working within the set confines of what society thinks men should wear."

How do fashion designers or brands approach you?
"I've received invitations to shows and after-parties, as well as store promotions and shopping exclusives. I'm really happy that PR professionals for brands recognise the importance of bloggers for their clients and make it a point to work closely with us bloggers."

Is your blog a step-up to working in the fashion industry?
"I'm considering working in marketing and communications in the fashion industry. I don't view my blog so much a step-up as a tool to motivate me to keep constantly *au courant* with what's happening in fashion."

What has been your most remarkable moment as a blogger so far?
"Being mentioned by Robbie Spencer of DAZED & CONFUSED as one of the blogs he regularly reads in an interview he did for MYKROMAG."

MODE PARADE

A look at MODE PARADE will tell you a thing or two about its writer. He is unusually eloquent, especially for a blogger, ever the gentleman, and he takes a special interest in fashion history. Suffice it to say: you're not dealing with your average twenty-something here. Born in London by Ghanaian parents, Barima Vox, or Barima Owusu-Nyantekyi as he is formally known as, went through the British boarding school system and graduated from the University of Manchester early in the 2000s. Besides maintaining his blog, which he describes as a 'sartorial and pop culture dissection column', Mr. Vox currently works as a freelance style journalist and communication specialist, splitting his time between Ghana and the UK. His unique personal style, which you might say contains a fair dose of 'dandyism,' was influenced mainly by his parents. "I was born the son of two medical professionals and business-people, and their conception of luxury and the finer things irrevocably shaped my outlook on high-end products and the usefulness of a polished appearance."

What role does blogging occupy in your daily life?
"Blogging allows me to indulge my passions for writing and exploring the margins and potentialities of personal style and popular culture. As a 'Style Journalist', I get to discuss these with people I meet through social occasions, which then engenders chats about details of clothes. It's refreshing to find out that more fellows notice and consider the effects of correct and interesting appearance on others. Half of my male friends know exactly how to dress for weddings, so credit where it's due."

In what way have your Ghanaian origins influenced your style and taste?
"The chieftains of the tribe we're from, the Ashanti, favour heavy gold accessories and finely woven, colourful, patterned, textured cloths with lots of drape. I believe this taste for finery has had a certain influence."

Do you feel like you were born in the wrong time period?
"I don't have any regrets about being born in the 1980s. Over the past two decades, I've seen boundaries broken and history made, and those are amongst the true values of the moment one lives in. The eras of the past I like wouldn't necessarily have allowed me to live the way I do now; socio-cultural restrictions and the non-existence of the internet are two burdens I'd rather not shoulder. That said, I'd have loved to have

BLOG TITLE
Mode Parade

URL
www.barimavox.blogspot.com

EDITOR
Barima Owusu-Nyantekyi

YEAR OF BIRTH
1982

ONLINE SINCE
February 2009

COUNTRY
UK

LANGUAGE
English

POSTS PER WEEK
1-3

VISITORS PER DAY
100

TAGS
pop culture, sartorialism

FAVOURITE BLOGS
www.venividivrai.blogspot.com
+
www.dandyism.net
+
www.maxminimus.blogspot.com
+
www.mostexerent.tumblr.com
+
www.thegrumpyowl.com

by Elina Tozzi

frequented or even worked in some of the Peacock/Mod establishments during the late 1960s, visited Paris in the Decadent Period, or studied under the Impressionists."

Do you consider yourself a dandy?
"Some consider me a dandy; others consider me something different and possibly new. And a third sector simply wants to know what I'm smoking and how to avoid it. Dandyism as a lifestyle is a total package; it's about dressing with consummate elegance and knowledge, with varying doses of creativity, iconoclasm and artistry. I can easily rule myself out. I don't own a beautiful dressing gown and slippers; my language and prose are not consistently refined; I sometimes go for days without shaving, and most of my accessories contain no precious metals. I'm also not irresponsible enough. I find 'offbeat formality' to be the best label to describe myself, since it accounts for both my dressed up attributes and my influences, from my Ghanaian roots to dapper Gilded Age dancers; from the Peacock Revolution to *louche* lounge lizards and mid-20th century businessmen, politicians and diplomats."

Do you have a specific reader group in mind when you blog?
"The beauty of MODE PARADE is that there's never been a fixed group. I was surprised to discover that women like it, for example. MODE PARADE is meant to be inspirational; as I continue to learn more about the clothes I champion, it will hopefully grow in a more educational manner. My outfit shots in particular are aimed at men who think dressing up is stuffy or antiquated or, more ridiculously, 'metro' and devoid of fun. I also aim it at potential like-minds; I'd enjoy meeting people who truly go against the current grain and set their own styles. Obsessive nerd types with allegiances to different forms of culture and admirable self-confidence; the types who don't care what others think of them and are all the better for it. "

How specifically does the male perspective on fashion blogging differ from a female one?
"The men's style blogs I read are rooted in exploring the minutiae, context, and history of tailored clothes. That is combined with examinations of their icons and recommendations of makers of quality. They're very much about building a wardrobe, focusing on particular garments more so than overall looks. Womenswear is different precisely because it's rooted more strongly in seasonal change, so its observers pay more attention to particular designers and 'It' items."

Where do you see yourself in ten years?
"In ten years, I'd like to have worked in branding for a leading communications firm or high-end luxury company. I also hope I'll have written something of true worth by then, as well as having learned more languages, a musical instrument, and how to juggle."

BLOG
INDEX

NEWS & VIEWS

BLOG TITLE	URL	TAGS	COUNTRY
A Cup of Jo	www.joannagoddard.blogspot.com	lifestyle, diary	USA
A Few Goody Gumdrops	www.afewgoodygumdrops.com	shopping	USA
A New Muse	www.anewmuse.net	designers, street style, shopping	AUS
A Wee Bit Skint	www.aweebitskint.com	shopping, trends, runway	CAN
Abdul Lagerfield	www.abdul-lagerfield.blogspot.com	diary, runway	NL
All Things Ordinary	www.allthingsordinary.net	runway, inspiration, diary	USA
An AUSn Wintour	www.anaustralianwintour.com	trends, celebrities	AUS
Animal Talk	www.theanimaltalk.blogspot.com	art, designers, pop culture	USA
Anmutig	www.anmutig.blogspot.com	designers, design, DIY	DE
Anywho	www.anywho.dk	trends, street style, shopping	DK
Araks	www.araks.com/blog	art, design, designers	USA
AthensWears	www.athenswears.com/	street style, night life	GR
AUS Style	www.ausstyle.blogspot.com	diary, designers, design	AUS
Awkward Digressions	www.awkwarddigressions.blogspot.com	diary, shopping, pop culture	AUS
Because im addicted	becauseimaddicted.net	designers, inspiration, shopping	USA
Ben Trovato	www.bentrovatoblog.com	inspiration, photography, designers	NOR
Black Magic	www.alittleblackmagic.blogspot.com	inspiration, designers	USA
Bleach Black	www.bleachblack.com	trends, designers, shopping	USA
Blue is in Fashion this Year	www.blueisinfashionthisyear.com	trends	I
Bored&Beautiful	blog.styleserver.de	runway, designers, trends	DE
Brains and Beauty	www.brainsbeauty.wordpress.com	trends, shopping	UK
Bryan Boy	www.bryanboy.com	diary, designers	PHL
Bunny BISOUS	www.julialapin.typepad.com	designers	USA
Café Mode	blogs.lexpress.fr/cafe-mode	street style	F
Capture the Castle	www.capturethecastle1.blogspot.com	designers, shopping, inspiration	AUS
Cat Party	www.ilovecatparty.blogspot.com	inspiration, pop culture	USA
Catwalk Queen	www.catwalkqueen.tv	trends, shopping, designers	UK
Chic & Untroubled	www.chicanduntroubled.com	shopping, trends, pop culture	USA
Coco's Tea Party	www.cocosteaparty.blogspot.com	celebrities, runway, trends	UK
CocoPerez	www.cocoperez.com	celebrities	USA
Code for Something	www.codeforsomething.com	photography, design, diary	NZ
Cookie Jar	www.thecookie-jar.blogspot.com	designers, trends	I
Cool & Chic	www.coolandchic.blogspot.com	inspiration, runway, celebrities	ES
Coûte que Coûte	www.coutequecoute.blogspot.com	runway, inspiration	DE
Delinlee Delovely	www.linleeloves.blogspot.com	diary, night life	USA
DenimHunt	www.denimhunt.com	shopping, designers	USA
Descolex	www.descolex.com	pop culture, trends	BRA
Detroit to Brooklyn	www.detroittobrooklyn.blogspot.com	street style, pop culture	US
Devil Wears Zara	www.devilwearszara.elleblogs.es	trends, celebrities, shopping	ES
Diane, A Shaded View on Fashion	www.ashadedviewonfashion.com	diary, designers	F
Die Young, Stay Pretty	www.dieyoungstaypretty88.wordpress.com	inspiration	UK
Dirtyflaws	www.dirtyflaws.com	inspiration, shopping, goth	USA
Disneyrollergirl	www.disneyrollergirl.blogspot.com	shopping, pop culture	UK
Dream Sequins	www.dreamsequins.com	designers, trends	USA

BLOG TITLE	URL	TAGS	COUNTRY
Dus*****infernus	www.dusinfernus.wordpress.com	runway, backstage, designers	BRA
El Fashionista	www.elfashionista.net	designers	ES
European Luxury Blog	www.europeanluxuryblog.com	designers	CH
F.A.D. (Fashion Addict Diary)	www.hotbisexualmodel.blogspot.com	pop culture, designers	USA
f&art	www.fartguide.blogspot.com	art, designers	DE
Fash-Eccentric!	www.fash-eccentric.com/	celebrities, shopping, designers	SG
Fashion Ambition	www.fashionambitions.blogspot.com	diary, backstage, runway	UK
Fashion Gone Rogue	www.fashiongonerogue.com	advertisement, magazines	USA
Fashion is Spinach	www.fashionisspinach.com/	shopping, diary, vintage	USA
Fashion Me Fabulous	www.fashionmefabulous.blogspot.com	beauty, shopping	USA
Fashion Reality	www.fashionreality.blogspot.com	inspiration, runway, celebrities	ES
Fashion Tidbits	www.fashion-tidbits.blogspot.com	inspiration, celebrities, designers	KOR
Fashion156	www.fashion156.com/blog.php	designers, trends	UK
Fashionalities	www.fashionalities.blogspot.com	shopping, diary	USA
Fashionfindsuk	www.fashionfindsuk.blogspot.com	shopping, designers, celebrities	UK
Fashionista	www.fashionista.com	pop culture, collage	USA
Fashionologie	www.fashionologie.com	designers, celebrities	USA
Fashiontribes	www.fashiontribes.typepad.com	trends, beauty, shopping	USA
Fat Fashion Assistant	www.fatfashionassistant.blogspot.com	diary, designers	UK
FeetManSeoul	www.feetmanseoul.com	news	KOR
Flora's Box	www.florasbox.blogspot.com	designers, inspiration	DE/AT
Frankfurt Fashion	www.frankfurtfashion.blogspot.com	pop culture, night life	DE
Frockwriter	www.frockwriter.blogspot.com	designers, models	AUS
Frugal Fashionista	www.frugal-fashionistas.com	shopping, trends, celebrities	USA
Geometric Sleep	www.geometricsleep.com	runway, magazines	USA
Get Your Plane Right on Time	www.getyourplanerightontime.com	street style, diary, pop culture	NL
Hanneli Mustaparta	www.hanneli.carousel.no	photography, outfits, diary	NOR
Happy People Don't Complain	www.happypeopledontcomplain.blogspot.com	pop culture, night life	IDN
Hapsical	www.hapsical.blogspot.com	designers, runway	UK
High Fashion Girl	www.highfashiongirl.com	shopping, designers, diary	USA
Hint Blog	www2.hintmag.com/department/hint-blog	designers, news	USA
Holier than Now	www.holierthannow.com	trends, designers, inspiration	USA
HopeHope	www.hopehope.ch	shopping, design	CH
Hotspot	www.hotspot.webblogg.se	trends, designers, shopping	SWE
I Blog Fashion	www.iblogfashion.blogspot.com	shopping	EIR
Igor + Andre	www.igorandandre.blogspot.com	illustration	USA
Is Mental	www.is-mental.blogspot.com	designers, trends, runway	USA
Isaac Likes	www.isaaclikes.com	backstage, interviews, opinion	NZ
July Stars	www.julystars.blogspot.com	diary, designers, inspiration	UK
Kingdom of Style	www.kingdomofstyle.typepad.co.uk	outfits, shopping	UK
Knight cat	www.knighttcat.com	photography, outfits, diary	USA
La Carmina	www.lacarmina.com/blog	goth, diary, pop culture	USA/JP
Lalila	www.lalila.de	designers, shopping	DE
Late Boots	www.lateboots.blogspot.com	pop culture, designers, night life	USA
Le Fashion	www.lefashionimage.blogspot.com	photography, magazines, inspiration	USA
Le Tang	tangz.blogbus.com	inspiration	CN
Les Mads	www.lesmads.de	shopping, designers	DE
Market Publique	blog.marketpublique.com	shopping, vintage, web shop	USA
Marquis de Lannes	www.marquisdelannes.com	runway, designers, models	F
Mo Veld	www.moveld.com	designers, inspiration	NL
modebeitrag	www.modebeitrag.de	designers, runway, journalism	DE
Montreal In Style	www.montreal-instyle.blogspot.com	street style, shopping	CAN
My Boyfriend is Very Sexy	pandagugu.blogbus.com	inspiration, designers	CN

BLOG TITLE	URL	TAGS	COUNTRY
Nicola Formichetti	www.nicolaformichetti.blogspot.com	photography, diary, celebrities	UK
Nitro:licious	www.nitrolicious.com	shopping, pop culture, celebrities	USA
Nuvonova	www.nuvonova.blogspot.com	art, shopping, DIY	UK
Observation Mode	www.observationmode.blogspot.com	shopping, accessories	USA
Omiru	www.omiru.com	shopping, trends	USA
P.S. - I made this	www.psimadethis.com	DIY, collage, accessories	USA
Painfully Hip	www.painfullyhip.com	diary, inspiration, trends	USA
Pillole di Moda	www.pilloledimoda.blogspot.com	inspiration, shopping, accessories	UK
Pink Rock Candy	www.pinkrockcandy.net	trends, shopping	USA
Playground&Imperfection	www.playgroundimperfection.blogspot.com	trends, designers	UK
Project Beltway	www.projectbeltway.com	night life	USA
Racked NY	www.racked.com	designers, shopping	USA
Random Fashion Coolness	www.randomfashioncoolness.com	collage, trends, inspiration	UK
Ropa Vieja	www.jesicola.blogspot.com	inspiration, trends, design	USA
She Breathes	www.shebreathes.com	shopping, designers	USA
Shefinds	www.shefinds.com	shopping, designers	USA
Shiny Squirrel	www.shinysquirrel.typepad.com	inspiration, design	USA
Should be on the Nanny	www.shouldbeonthenanny.blogspot.com	pop culture, designers	USA
Simplyolive	www.simplyolive.blogspot.com	designers, runway	USA
So Fash'on	www.sofashon.com	DIY, designers, diary	ROM
So Long As It Is Black	www.solongasitisblack.com	designers	DK
Style Bubble	www.stylebubble.co.uk	outfits, designers	UK
Style File	www.style.com/stylefile	designers, celebrities	USA
Style On Track	www.styleontrack.com	street style, pop culture, inspiration	AUS
Style Tabloid	www.styletab.blogspot.com	trends, shopping, accessories	USA
Style Voyeur	www.stylevoyeur.com	night life, diary, street style	AUS
StyleJunkee	www.stylejunkee.com	shopping, beauty	UK
Super Sneaky Street Scene	www.supersneakystreetscene.blogspot.com	magazines, runway	ZA
Surabaya Fashion Carnival	www.sbyfashioncarnival.blogspot.com	street style, outfits	IDN
The Apathist	www.theapathist.blogspot.com	inspiration, pop culture	UK
The Business of Fashion	www.businessoffashion.com	designers, lifestyle	UK
The City Loves You	www.thecitylovesyou.com/fashion	shopping, pop culture	MEX
The Cool Hunter	www.thecoolhunter.net	shopping, lifestyle	USA
The Coveted	www.the-coveted.com	shopping, designers	USA
The Danettes	www.thedanettes.typepad.com	design, designers, lifestyle	DK
The Digitalistas	www.thedigitalistas.com	designers, shopping	NL
The Fashion Setter	www.thefashionsetter.blogspot.com	shopping, magazines, designers	I
The Fashionable Housewife	www.thefashionablehousewife.com	shopping, beauty	USA
The Imagist	www.theimagist.com	designers, inspiration	USA
The Intersection	www.the-intersection.blogspot.com	street style, night life, designers	USA
The Musings of Ondo Lady	www.themusingsofondolady.blogspot.com	pop culture, lifestyle	UK
The Pretty Pear	www.prettypear.com	shopping, plus size	USA
The Style PA	www.thestylepa.com	shopping, trends, beauty	UK
The Swelle Life	www.theswellelife.com	designers, trends, food	UK
Tongue in Chic	www.tonguechic.com	street style	MYS
Trend de la Crème	www.trenddelacreme.com	shopping, trends, accessories	USA
Très Plus Cool	www.trespluscool.com	design	DE
Urban Updater	www.urbanupdater.wordpress.com	shopping, trends, celebrities	USA
Wardrobe Wisdom	www.wardrobewisdom.blogspot.com	designers, shopping, diary	UK
We Are the Market	www.wearethemarket.com	shopping, lifestyle	USA
William Yan	www.williamyan.com	diary, street style	USA
With Asian Stereotypes	www.pigeonwithamonocle.blogspot.com	goth, designers, inspiration	USA
Ytligheter	www.ytligheter.com	diary, outfits, shopping	SWE

SEEN ON
THE STREETS

BLOG TITLE	URL	TAGS	COUNTRY
Advanced Style	www.advancedstyle.blogspot.com	advanced, chic, classic	USA
All the Pretty Birds	www.alltheprettybirds.blogspot.com	diary, trends	I
Altamira: Models Off Duty	www.altamiranyc.blogspot.com	models	USA
Antwerp Fashion Observer	www.antwerpfashionobserver.blogspot.com	chic, urban	BE
Apparel web	www.apparel-web.com/trend	urban	JP
Appeal to the Eye	www.appealtotheeye.blogspot.com	pop culture	ES
Austin style watch	www.austinstylewatch.com	news, pop culture	USA
Backyard Bill	www.backyardbill.com	menswear, portraits	USA
Broad&Market	www.cyborgmemoirs.com/street	portraits	USA
Budapest Style	www.lookz.hu/budapest-style	urban	HU
Chicago Looks	www.chicagolooks.blogspot.com	night life	USA
Click/clash	www.clickclash.blogspot.com	night life	USA
Copenhagen Cycle Chic	www.copenhagencyclechic.com	chic, bikes	DK
CopenhagenStreetStyle	www.copenhagenstreetstyle.dk	classic, portraits	DK
Dam Style	www.damstyle.blogspot.com	portraits, vintage	NL
Deep City Dive	www.deepcitydive.blogspot.com	pop culture, night life	MEX
Dropstitch	www.dropstitch.com.au	news, runway	AUS
Dublin Streets	www.dublinstreets.blogspot.com	night life	EIR
Easy Fashion	www.easyfashion.blogspot.com	chic, portraits	F
Face Hunter	www.facehunter.blogspot.com	chic, trends, portraits	UK
FadTony	www.fadtony.blogspot.com	portraits	NL
Fashion Filosofy	www.fashionfilosofy.com	night life, news	EIR
Gademode	www.gademode.dk	chic, details	DK
Garance Doré	www.garancedore.fr	diary, illustration, portraits	F
Hel Looks	www.hel-looks.com	colours, portraits	FIN
HiStyley	www.histyley.com	chic, classic	USA
Hoy Fashion	www.hoyfashion.co.uk	details, trends	UK
I Got Shot in the City	www.igotshotinthecity.vox.com	basic, details	MYS
ILook	israblog.nana.co.il/ilook	colours, urban	ISR
Jak & Jil	www.jakandjil.com	models, shoes	USA
Just Glitter Lust	www.justglitterlust.blogspot.com	chic, portraits	EST
Ljubljana Fashion Avenue	www.ljubljanafashionavenue.blogspot.com	urban	SI
Mess This Dress	www.messthisdress.blogspot.com	night life	MEX
Mister Mort	www.mistermort.typepad.com	menswear, trends	USA
Modedorf	www.modedorf.blogspot.com	chic, classic	DE
Mr. Newton	www.mrnewton.net	night life, news	USA
Naples Streetstyle	www.naplestreetstyle.it	night life	I
Nowhere to go - Nothing to do	www.nowheretogo-nothingtodo.blogspot.com	night life	NZ
O Alfaiate Lisboeta	www.oalfaiatelisboeta.blogspot.com	classic, menswear	PT
On the Corner	www.onthecorner.com.ar	urban	ARG
Pics by Polka Dot	www.streetstylelondon.blogspot.com	diary	UK
PimPumPam	www.pimpumpam.blogspot.com	portraits	I
Plastic Choko	www.plasticchoko.blogspot.com	outfits, trends	I
Rio etc.	www.rioetc.blogspot.com	news, outfits	BRA

BLOG TITLE	URL	TAGS	COUNTRY
São Paulo Style	www.saopaulostyle.blogspot.com	night life	BRA
Show Me Your Wardrobe	www.showmeyourwardrobe.blogspot.com	outfits, portraits	UK
Stil in Berlin	www.stilinberlin.blogspot.com	portraits	DE
StockholmStreetStyle	stockholmstreetstyle.feber.se	models, trends	SWE
Street Peeper	www.streetpeeper.com	worldwide	USA
Streetgeist	www.streetgeist.com	colours, trends	GR
Streetstyle Aesthetic	www.waynetippetts.com	details, portraits	UK
Style and the City	www.styleandthecity.com	models	F
Style Defined	www.styledefined.blogspot.com	night life	USA
Style du Monde	www.lovedistortion.com/styledumonde	basic, classic	BE
Style from Tokyo	stylefromtokyo.blogspot.com	classic, trends	JP
Style Slicker	styleslicker.wordpress.com	diary, models	UK
Style-arena	www.style-arena.jp/en	shopping, colours	JP
Styleclicker	www.styleclicker.net	chic, portraits	DE
Stylesightings	www.stylesightings.com	details, models, trends	USA
Styletracker	www.style-tracker.blogspot.com	night life	SWE
Stylites in Beijing	www.stylites.net	details, news	CN
Textstyles	www.torontotextstyles.blogspot.com	news, lifestyle	CAN
The Fashionist	www.thefashionist.se	details, trends	SWE
The Manfattan Project	www.themanfattanproject.tumblr.com	plus size	USA
The MidWasteland	www.themidwasteland.com	men, classic	USA
The Minneapoline	www.theminneapoline.blogspot.com	basic, classic	USA
The Pregnant Goldfish	www.pregnantgoldfish.wordpress.com	night life	CAN
The Sartorialist	www.thesartorialist.blogspot.com	classic, chic, portraits	USA
The SF Style	www.thesfstyle.com	diary	USA
The Stitch Society	www.stitchsociety.blogspot.com	lifestyle	USA
The Streethearts	www.thestreethearts.com	classic, chic, portraits	NOR
The Streets Walker	www.thestreetswalker.blogspot.com	urban, colours	ISR
The Style Scout	www.stylescout.blogspot.com	vintage, basic	UK
The Style Tyrant	www.thestyletyrant.com	men, portraits	AUS
Tokyo Bopper	www.tokyobopper.com	shopping, trends	JP
Toronto street fashion	www.torontostreetfashion.com	trends, night life	CAN
Tragflaeche Leipzig	www.tragflaeche-leipzig.de	interviews	DE
Turned Out	www.turnedout.tv/index.php	collages, portraits	USA
Über Brum	www.uberbrum.blogspot.com	night life	UK
Ugly Outfits New York	www.uglyoutfitsnyc.com	ugly, celebrities	USA
Ukraine Street Fashion	www.street-style.com.ua	trends	UKR
Vaquum	www.vaquum.org	aggregator, worldwide	JP
Vanessa Jackman	www.vanessajackman.blogspot.com	models	UK
Xssat	www.xssat.wordpress.com	details, colours	AUS
Your Boyhood	www.yourboyhood.com	art, news	KOR

PERSONAL STYLE DIARIES

BLOG TITLE	URL	TAGS	COUNTRY
10.17	www.tenseventen.blogspot.com	inspiration, outfits, diary	USA
4th and Bleeker	www.4thandbleekeragency.blogspot.com	diary, models, web shop	USA
A Cat of Impossible Colour	www.acatofimpossiblecolour.blogspot.com	outfits, diary, vintage	NZ
A Clock Without Hands	www.aclockwithouthands.blogspot.com	diary, inspiration	USA
A Curious Seamstress	www.acuriousseamstress.blogspot.com	DIY, vintage, web shop	USA
A Red Lipstick	www.a-red-lipstick.blogspot.com	vintage, inspiration, diary	NOR
A Slowboat to Mediocrity	www.hihosilvero.blogspot.com	art, inspiration	JP
Africana Wardrobe Diary	www.africanainatlanta.blogspot.com	outfits, shopping	USA
Afroboheme	www.afroboheme.blogspot.com	outfits, shopping, inspiration	F
Agent Lover	www.agentlover.com/blog	pop culture, outfits	USA
Aifowy	www.aifowy.blox.pl	outfits, shopping	POL
Alexandra Grecco	www.gludafindslulu.blogspot.com	vintage, inspiration, diary	USA
Alice Point	www.alicepoint.blogspot.com	outfits, diary, shopping	POL
Allure-Allure	www.allure-allure.blogspot.com	outfits, inspiration, pop culture	ES
Alma H	www.aperfectguide.se/almah	outfits, diary, designers	SWE
Amlul	www.amlul.com	diary, outfits	UK
Annie Spandex	www.anniespandex.com	outfits, diary, pop culture	USA
Atlantis Home	www.atlantishome.typepad.com	diary, outfits, accessories	USA
Bear	www.raben-schwarz.blogspot.com	outfits, art, poetry	DE
Bees and Ballons	www.beesandballons.blogspot.com	outfits, shopping, designers	DE
Behind the Seams	www.theseams.blogspot.com	outfits, shopping, diary	USA
Betty Lou got a new...	www.bettylougotanew.blogspot.com	vintage, shopping, diary	SWE
Big Daddy	www.bigdadddy.blogspot.com	outfits, diary	USA
Blondinbella	www.blondinbella.se	diary, shopping	SWE
Blushing Ambition	www.blushingambition.blogspot.com	food, diary, outfits	USA
Bohemian Musings	www.bohememusings.blogspot.com	outfits, diary, inspiration	DE
Bonjour Adieu	www.bonjouradieu.blogspot.com	outfits, shopping	USA
Bookofmiri	www.bookofmiri.blogg.se	outfits, diary	SWE
Casey's Elegant Musings	blog.caseybrowndesigns.com	vintage, DIY, inspiration	USA
Charlize Mystery	www.charlize-mystery.blogspot.com	outfits, shopping, trends	POL
Cheapskate Chic	www.cheapskatechic.blogspot.com	outfits, shopping, inspiration	UK
Check Out	www.sovituskopissa.blogspot.com	outfits, diary	FIN
Childhood Flames	www.childhoodflames.blogspot.com	outfits, diary, shopping	USA
Chloé Van Paris	www.chloevanparis.blogspot.com	vintage, inspiration, pop culture	F
Chronically Vintage	www.chronicallyvintage.com	vintage, inspiration, shopping	CAN
Cinderella	www.jennycindy.blogspot.com	diary, outfits, runway	CH
Cindiddy	www.cindiddy.com	outfits, diary	CN
Clever Nettle	www.clevernettle.com/blog	outfits, vintage, web shop	USA
Clothes, Cameras and Coffee	www.clothescamerasandcoffee.blogspot.com	outfits, inspiration, diary	UK
Cupcakes and Cashmere	www.cupcakesandcashmere.com	shopping, outfits, diary	USA
Daddy Likey	www.daddylikey.blogspot.com	diary, shopping	USA
Dear Nike	www.nikesofiaamorina.blogspot.com	inspiration, photography	SWE
Diamond Canopy	www.diamondcanopywinn.blogspot.com	diary, outfits	UK
DiamondHurts	www.diamondhurts.blogspot.com	diary, outfits, inspiration	IDN

BLOG TITLE	URL	TAGS	COUNTRY
Diary of a Vintage Girl	www.diaryofavintagegirl.blogspot.com	vintage, outfits, diary	UK
Dirty Laundry	www.dirtydirtylaundry.wordpress.com	outfits, designers, trends	CR
Dirty pretty things	www.dirty-prettythings.blogspot.com	outfits, diary, runway	JP
Dirtyglam	www.dirtyglam.blogg.se	diary, outfits	SWE
Discofunbath	www.discofunbath.blogspot.com	street style, inspiration, diary	USA
Discotheque Confusion	www.discothequeconfusion.blogspot.com	diary, outfits, inspiration	UK
Dollface is Candysweet	www.dollface-is-candysweet.blogspot.com	outfits, diary, plus size	UK
Dotti's dots	www.dottisdots.blogspot.com	outfits, diary, vintage	CH
Dream On	www.dreamon-blog.blogspot.com	outfits, diary, shopping	NL
Dreamecho	www.hello-dreamecho.blogspot.com	diary, shopping, outfits	USA
Dusty Dress	www.dustydress.blogspot.com	outfits, diary, shopping	SWE
Elenita	www.elenita.no	outfits, diary, inspiration	NOR
Elinkan	www.radarzine.com/blogg/elinkan	outfits, diary, inspiration	SWE
Ellinorak	www.ellinorak.blogg.se	diary, outfits	SWE
Emma Nygren	www.emmanygren.freshnet.se	diary, outfits	SWE
Everything is Nonsense	www.everything-is-nonsense.blogspot.com	diary, inspiration	UK
Fashion Architect	www.fashionarchitect.blogspot.com	diary, shopping, DIY	GR
Fashion Bananas	www.fashionbananas.com	outfits, shopping, diary	USA
Fashion Chalet	www.fashionchalet.blogspot.com	diary, outfits	USA
Fashion Diary	www.missleelu.blogspot.com	diary, shopping	DE
Fashion Flux	www.fashionflux.indiedays.com	diary, goth, outfits	FIN
Fashion for Writers	www.fashionforwriters.com	diary, outfits	USA
Fashion Forestry	www.fashionforestry.blogspot.com	outfits, DIY, vintage	USA
Fashion Hayley	www.fashionhayley.com	outfits, shopping, diary	AUS
Fashion Nation	www.fashionation.wordpress.com	inspiration, web shop, diary	IDN
Fashion Pirates	www.fashionpirates.blogspot.com	outfits, shopping, inspiration	USA
Fashion Squad	www.fashionsquad.com	shopping, inspiration, outfits	SWE
Fashion Toast	www.fashiontoast.com	outfits, shopping, diary	USA
Fashion Wrap	www.fashionwrap.blogspot.com	outfits, diary, web shop	AUS
Fashionnerdic	www.fashion-nerdic.blogspot.com	diary, outfits, shopping	NL
Fashionshot	www.fashionshot.blogspot.com	diary, outfits	DE
Fatshionable	www.fatshionable.com	shopping, outfits, plus size	USA
Filippas Mode	www.filippas.se	diary, outfits	SWE
Flora	www.florasblogg.se	diary	SWE
Flying Saucer	www.flyingsaucer.typepad.com	diary, shopping	UK
Foxyman	www.thefoxyman.blogspot.com	diary, outfits, pop culture	AUS
Frassy	www.befrassy.com	outfits, shopping, diary	UK
Fruchtzwerg's Island	www.fruchtzwergisland.blogspot.com	outfits, shopping	DE
Garbage Dress	www.garbagedress.blogspot.com	outfits, diary, night life	USA
Grey	www.greytheblog.com	news, design, diary	CAN
Growin' Up	www.growin--up.blogspot.com	diary, vintage, DIY	UK
Hand It Over	www.handmeover.blogspot.com	outfits, shopping, inspiration	USA
Hanna and Landon	www.hannahandlandon.blogspot.com	diary, nostalgic, vintage	USA
Happy Because	www.happy-because.blogspot.com	outfits, diary	UK
Heart in a Cage	www.ifyouweretherebeware.blogspot.com	inspiration, outfits, diary	NL
Here There and Back Again	www.samanthapleet.blogspot.com	diary, vintage, art	USA
Hold in your Breath	www.hold-in-your-breath.blogspot.com	inspiration, diary, outfits	NL
Hot Chocolate & Mint	www.dianarikasari.blogspot.com	outfits, diary, shopping	IDN
I need a dress	www.ineedadress.blogspot.com	diary, designers, outfits	NL
Imelda	www.i-melda.blogspot.com	outfits, diary, shopping	BE
It'll Take The Snap Out ...	www.snapped-garters.blogspot.com	vintage, outfits, DIY	USA
Jazzi McG	www.jazzimcg.com/blog	outfits, shopping, inspiration	USA
Julia	www.julia.blogg.se	outfits, diary	SWE

BLOG TITLE	URL	TAGS	COUNTRY
Kafferepet	www.miriamskafferep.blogspot.com	vintage, diary, outfits	SWE
Karla's Closet	www.karlascloset.blogspot.com	diary, outfits	USA
Karnaah	www.karnaah.devote.se	diary, outfits	SWE
Kelly	www.kellybiddle.se	diary, DIY	SWE
Kenza	www.kenzas.se	diary	SWE
Kirafashion	www.kirafashion.com.br	diary, outfits, shopping	BRA
Knight Cat	www.knighttcat.com	inspiration, models, shopping	USA
Kristin Prim	www.kristinprim.typepad.com	diary, outfits	USA
l'Atelier d'une Fée	www.latelierdunefee.fr	photography, outfits, DIY	F
Lacquer	www.condenasty.blogspot.com	shopping, outfits	USA
Lady Melbourne	www.ladymelbourne.blogspot.com	vintage, shopping, outfits	AUS
Le blog de betty	www.leblogdebetty.com	diary, outfits, DIY	F
Le blog mode de Mayahanna	www.mahayanna.wordpress.com	outfits	F
Le Monde de Tokyobanhbao	www.tokyobanhbao.com	diary, outfits	F
Le Style	www.lestyle.devote.se	diary, outfits	SWE
Lea Loves	www.lealoves.blogspot.com	diary, news	DE
LeeseLooks	www.leeselooks.blogspot.com	outfits, runway	CAN
Left hand endeavor	www.lefthandendeavor.blogspot.com	vintage, web shop, outfits	CAN
Lemonize	www.l-e-m-o-n-i-z-e.blogspot.com	inspiration, photography, outfits	NL
Libertylondongirl	www.libertylondongirl.com	diary, news	USA
Liebemarlene Vintage	www.liebemarlene.blogspot.com	diary, outfits, vintage	USA
Lily Satine	www.psychedeslys.wordpress.com	vintage, outfits	F
Linn	www.linngustafsson.se	shopping, news	SWE
Lions, Tigers & Fashion OH MY!	www.lionstigersandfashionohmy.com	diary, outfits, shopping	USA
Lisaplace	www.lisaplace.devote.se	outfits, shopping	SWE
Little Sneak into my Life	www.nita-karoliina.blogspot.com	diary, outfits	USA
Lola is Beauty	www.lolaisbeauty.blogspot.com	diary, food	UK
Loose Leaf Tigers	www.looseleaftigers.blogspot.com	vintage, inspiration	CAN
LoveMore	www.lovemoreblog.blogspot.com	outfits, diary, shopping	AUS
Loveology	www.mila-loveology.blogspot.com	diary, photography	NL
Madame Mode	www.madamemode.blogspot.com	outfits, diary, inspiration	NL
Madame Says	www.madamesays.com	diary, pop culture	UK
Mahalo Fashion	www.mahalofashion.blogspot.com	celebrities, inspiration, runway	CAN
Make it Work!	www.coffeefashionandtv.blogspot.com	diary, outfits	DE
Mallrat Couture	www.mallratcouture.blogspot.com	outfits, shopping	CAN
Matildas Delights	www.missmatildadreams.blogspot.com	vintage, diary, shopping	UK
M. & m. m. of the m.-esque me's	www.thevagabondset.com/blog	inspiration	UK
Miss at la Playa	www.missatlaplaya.blogspot.com	inspiration, news	ES
Miss Couturable	www.misscouturable.com	shopping, diary, outfits	USA
Miss Wink	www.misswink.blogspot.com	vintage, inspiration	SWE
Mode Rapide	www.moderapide.blogspot.com	outfits, art, design	CAN
Moderniteter	www.modette.se/moderniteter/blogg	diary, outfits, vintage	SWE
Mollywood	www.mollywood-blog.blogspot.com	diary, inspiration	DK
Montmarte's Sketchbook	www.montmarte.blogspot.com	diary, DIY, design	USA
Musings of a Fatshionista	blog.musingsofafatshionista.com	plus size, outfits, shopping	USA
My Daily Style	www.mydailystyle.es	outfits, news	ES
My Favorite Color is Shiny	www.ginnybranch.blogspot.com	diary, photography	USA
My Floor is Red	www.myfloorisred.com	trends, shopping, outfits	I
Next-Trend	www.next-trend.com	shopping, outfits	F
Nice and Shiny	www.niceandshiny.blogspot.com	outfits, shopping	CAN
niotillfem	www.rodeo.net/niotillfem	diary, outfits	SWE
Nothing Elegant	www.nothing-elegant.blogspot.com	inspiration	USA
Nuvonova	www.nuvonova.blogspot.com	art, design	UK

BLOG TITLE	URL	TAGS	COUNTRY
Oh Elle	www.ohelle.blogspot.com	diary, outfits, inspiration	UK
On dressing up	www.ondressingup.blogspot.com	outfits, diary	NZ
Origami mon ami	www.origamimonami.blogspot.com	news, design	BE
Outsapop Trashion	www.outsapop.com	inspiration	FIN
Owl and the Grapes	www.owlandthegrapes.blogspot.com	outfits, inspiration	AUS
Panda Fuck	www.thepandafck.de	outfits, inspiration	DE
Pandora	www.misspandora.fr	inspiration, art	F
Park & Cube	www.parkandcube.com	outfits, DIY, jewelry	UK
Perisacooper	www.perisacooper.blogspot.com	outfits, diary, shopping	SG
PersonalShopper	www.yourprivateshopper.blogspot.com	outfits, shopping	F
Phosphene	www.phosphenefashion.com	outfits, DIY, runway	USA
pick a flower	www.not-a-doll.blogspot.com	shopping, outfits, diary	NL
Picked Pics	www.pickedpics.blogspot.com	diary, outfits	DE
Polkadots & Vodkashots	www.polkadots-vodkashots.blogspot.com	diary, photography	NOR
Prêt à Porter P	www.pretaporterp.blogspot.com	outfits, trends, diary	USA
Pretty In Black	www.realprettyinblack.blogspot.com	inspiration	USA
Pretty Little Pictures	www.the-paperdoll.blogspot.com	outfits, webshop, diary	NZ
Pretty Pirate Designs	www.prettyprettypirate.blogspot.com	web shop, shopping, outfits	USA
Professionaly Trendy	www.professionally-trendy.blogspot.com	news, trends, inspiration	CAN
Pudri	www.pudri.blogspot.com	news, art	DE
Punky B's Fashion Diary	www.punky-b.com	diary, outfits	F
Punky style	www.punkystyle.com	shopping, outfits, web shop	USA
Ragnhild	www.ragnhild.blogg.se	outfits, inspiration	SWE
Rantings of a Fashion Addict	www.rantingsofafashionaddict.blogspot.com	diary, outfits	CAN
Raver Ria	www.raverria.blogspot.com	shopping, photography, inspiration	AUS
Renée Sturme/blog	www.fashionfillers.com	outfits, shopping, diary	NL
Restée Rêveuse	www.boutdelu.blogspot.com	photography, illustration	F
Righteous (re)Style	www.righteousrestyle.com	eco, shopping, trends	USA
Ringo, have a banana	www.ringohaveabanana.blogspot.com	inspiration	USA
Rosa-Fiona Bettina	www.pixieyou.blogspot.com	outfits, diary, shopping	FIN
Rosie Pop	www.rosiepop.typepad.com	news, pop culture	UK
Runaway Gallery	www.runawaygallery.com	diary, outfits	USA
Sally Jane Vintage	www.sallyjanevintage.blogspot.com	diary, outfits, vintage	USA
Scout holiday	www.scout-holiday.com/blog	photography, design, inspiration	USA
Sea of Shoes	www.seaofshoes.typepad.com	diary, outfits, accessories	USA
Sequin Magazine	www.sequinmagazine.blogspot.com	diary, outfits	EST
She's in Fashion	www.elle.se/bloggar/filippa-bergs-blogg.aspx	diary, outfits	SWE
She's in Vogue	www.shesinvogue.blogspot.com	inspiration, outfits, trends	EIR
Sidewalks are Runways	www.sidewalksarerunways.blogspot.com	outfits, diary, shopping	USA
Sighsandwhispers	www.sighswhispers.blogspot.com	vintage, photography, web shop	USA
Sigrid	www.popthatcork.devote.se	diary, food	SWE
Sincerely, Jules	www.sincerelyjules.blogspot.com	news, inspiration	USA
Six Six Sick	www.sixsixsick.blogspot.com	diary, outfits, shopping	USA
Sleep D. and S. of My Bullshit Youth	www.gnarlitude.com	shopping, outfits, pop culture	USA
Something Picasso	www.thesomethingpicasso.blogspot.com	outfits	USA
Somewhere Here	www.vintage-tea.blogspot.com	vintage, diary, inspiration	UK
song of style	www.songofstyle.com	outfits, models	USA
Sonia Fashion Box	www.sonia-fashionbox.com	outfits, trends, shopping	F
Sophie's Fashion	www.sophiesfashion.blogg.se	shopping, celebrities	SWE
Starbucks and Jane Austen	www.starbucksandjane.blogspot.com	inspiration, celebrities, shopping	CAN
Stella's Wardrobe	www.stellaswardrobe.blogspot.com	outfits	UK
Stud Farm	www.studfarmer.blogspot.com	diary, shopping	AUS
Style by Kling	stylebykling.tv4.se	diary, outfits	SWE

BLOG TITLE	URL	TAGS	COUNTRY
Style Discovery	www.stylediscovery.com.au	runway, inspiration	AUS
Style High Club	www.stylehighclub.wordpress.com	diary, inspiration, vintage	UK
Style Hurricane	www.stylehurricane.blogspot.com	outfits, DIY, jewelry	EST
Style Lines	www.stylelines.blogspot.com	news, designers	UK
Style...A Work In Progress	www.styleawip.blogspot.com	diary, outfits, shopping	USA
Stylediger	www.stylediger.blogspot.com	diary, outfits	POL
Super Kawaii Mama	www.superkawaiimama.com	outfits, web shop, vintage	AUS
Szafa Sztywniary	www.szafasztywniary.blogspot.com	diary, outfits	POL
Taghrid	www.taghrid.cc	outfits, photography	USA
That's Chic	www.thatschic.blogspot.com	diary, outfits, photography	USA
The Cherry Blossom Girl	www.thecherryblossomgirl.com	diary, outfits, shopping	F
The Cupcake Diary	www.thecupcakediary.blogspot.com	diary, inspiration	I
The Fashion Press	www.thefashionpress.blogspot.com	outfits, news	CAN
The Freelancer's Fashionblog	www.freelancersfashion.blogspot.com	outfits, diary, vintage	FIN
The Glamorous Librarian	www.glambibliotekaren.blogspot.com	vintage, inspiration, shopping	NOR
The Glamourai	www.theglamourai.com	outfits, inspiration, street style	USA
The Lake of One's Being	www.thehipsterparade.blogspot.com	diary, inspiration	SG
The Neverending Story!	www.saganendalausa.blogspot.com	outfits, diary, photography	UK
The New Black	www.thenewblack-starr.blogspot.com	outfits, diary	USA
The Snail and the Cyclops	www.thesnailandthecyclops.blogspot.com	vintage, web shop, outfits	USA
The Stylish Wanderer	www.thestylishwanderer.blogspot.com	outfits, diary	USA
This Chick's Got Style	www.thischicksgotstyle.blogspot.com	outfits, shopping, diary	NL
Thrills and Frills	www.thrillsandfrills.blogspot.com	shopping, outfits, trends	UK
Tjejsaiten	www.tjejsajten.blogspot.com	diary, inspiration	CAN
Toujours Amoureux	www.evolvlove.blogspot.com	diary	AUS
Trois Douze	www.trois-douze.blogspot.com	inspiration, shopping	NL
Ulrikke Lund	www.ulrikkelunds.blogg.no	trends, beauty, outfits	NOR
Unlimited Clothes	www.unlimited-clothes.blogspot.com	outfits, trends	BE
Vain and Vapid	www.vainandvapid.blogspot.com	shopping, web shop	USA
Valentsine	www.valentsine.blogspot.com	inspiration, shopping, diary	CAN
Vanillascented	www.vanillascented.freshnet.se	outfits, designers, shopping	NOR
Vintage Deerhunter	www.vintagedeerhunter.blogspot.com	diary, vintage, inspiration	SWE
Vintage is the new Black	www.noirohiovintage.blogspot.com	vintage, web shop, outfits	USA
Vintageportalen	www.vintageportalen.se	vintage, ouftits, diary	SWE
Vixen Vintage	www.vixenvintage.blogspot.com	vintage, diary	USA
Wartime Recess	www.wartimerecess.blogspot.com	inspiration, designers, outfits	USA
We Make it Work	www.wemakeitwork.de	diary, inspiration, pop culture	DE
What is Reality Anyway	www.whatisrealityanyway.com	outfits, diary	USA
WishWishWish	www.wishwishwish.net	outfits, vintage	UK
With My Style	www.silmukka-anni.blogspot.com	diary, inspiration	FIN
Your Private Shopper	www.yourprivateshopper.blogspot.com	trends, diary	F

CREATURES OF THE NIGHT

BLOG TITLE	URL	TAGS	COUNTRY
7daysisaweekend	www.7daysisaweekend.com	runway, pop culture, news	DE
Buvez Madison Journal	www.buvezmadison.blogspot.com	runway, pop culture, diary	F
Caesar Sebastian	www.caesarsebastian.com	pop culture	USA
Dance Right	www.danceright.net	street style, pop culture	USA
Darkroom Demons	www.darkroomdemons.com	pop culture	USA
Das Kind	www.daskind.nl	pop culture, news	NL
Deers and Bears	www.deersandbears.com	pop culture, diary	NZ
Diario de Fiestas	www.diariodefiestas.blogspot.com	designers	MEX
Driven By Boredom	www.drivenbyboredom.com	pop culture	USA
Everyoneisfamous	www.everyoneisfamous.com	pop culture, news	USA
Faceadelphia	www.faceadelphia.blogspot.com	street style, pop culture	USA
Freakstyle	www.freakstyle-freakstyle.blogspot.com	street style, designers	BRA
Glamcanyon	www.glamcanyon.blogspot.com	street style	UK
Glitter Guts	www.glitterguts.com	pop culture	USA
Hobo Gestapo	www.hobogestapo.com	street style	AUS
Icanteachyouhowtodoit	www.icanteachyouhowtodoit.com	street style, pop culture	ES
Kidpaparazzi	www.kidpaparazzi.com	pop culture	USA
La pola	www.lap0la.blogspot.com	pop culture	MEX
Lastnightsparty	www.lastnightsparty.com	pop culture	USA
Lindsaysdiet	www.lindsaysdiet.com	pop culture	USA
Misshapes	www.misshapes.com	pop culture, runway	USA
NefariousGirl	www.nefariousgirl.com	pop culture	USA
Neon Sleep	www.neonsleep.com	pop culture	NZ
Nicky Digital	www.nickydigital.com	pop culture, news	USA
Oh Snap Kid	www.ohsnapkid.com	news, shopping	USA
OutWithMe	www.outwithme.com	pop culture	USA
Playlust	www.playlust.net	street style, news	CH
Pretend it Never Happened	www.pretenditneverhappened.blogspot.com	pop culture	NL
Redslurpeee	www.redslurpeee.com	pop culture	USA
Rony's Photobooth	www.ronysphotobooth.com	pop culture	USA
Shadowscene	www.shadowscene.com/fiesta.html	pop culture	USA
Shark vs. Bear	www.sharkvsbear.com	pop culture	CAN
Smile for Camera	www.smileforcamera.com	pop culture, news	USA
Street Tease	www.street-tease.com/street-night	pop culture, news	F
Take More Photos	www.takemorephotos.com	photography	CAN
Takeover Tokyo	www.takeovertokyo.com	pop culture	USA
The CameROscope	www.thecameroscope.com	pop culture	F
The Cobra Snake	www.thecobrasnake.com	pop culture, runway	USA
The Culture of Me	www.thecultureofme.com	pop culture, news	USA
The Young Wolff Event Photography	www.theyoungwolff.blogspot.com	street style, pop culture	USA
We Are Awesome	www.we-are-awesome.com	street style, pop culture	ZA
WeKnowWhatYouDidLastNight	www.weknowwhatyoudidlastnight.com	designers, backstage	UK
Yapsnaps	www.yapsnaps.blogspot.com	diary	USA

WHAT ABOUT THE BOYS?

BLOG NAME	URL	TAGS	COUNTRY
00o00	www.00o00.blogspot.com	diary, shopping	UK
A Continuous Lean	www.acontinuouslean.com	shopping, designers	USA
A suitable wardrobe	www.asuitablewardrobe.dynend.com	history, menswear	USA
Bloke	www.blokemenswear.blogspot.com	opinion, trends	USA
Buckets and Spades	www.buckets-and-spades.blogspot.com	diary, shopping	UK
Cometothewildside	www.cometothewildside.blogspot.com	designers, outfits, shopping	DE
Dandy Gum	www.dandygum.blogspot.com	designers, art	F
Dennis M	www.dennism.se	diary, outfits	SWE
Fashion Bits and Bobs	www.fashionbitsandbobs.com	diary, street style	CH
He Breathes	www.hebreathes.com	diary, shopping, news	USA
I am hia	www.iamhia.blogspot.com	diary, photography	DE
Jake Davis Blog	www.jakedavis.typepad.com	inspiration, pop culture	USA
Jeaniuss	www.jeaniuss.blogspot.com	diary	NL
katelovesme	www.katelovesme.net	outfits, diary	UK/ES
Kempt	www.getkempt.com	grooming, trends	USA
Lame Basics	www.lamebasics.com	diary, shopping	USA
Le Vrai Winston	www.venividivrai.blogspot.com	outfits, shopping	UK
Maison Chaplin	www.maisonchaplin.blogspot.com	designers, diary	PT
Male Mode	www.male-mode.com	news, designers, shopping	EIR
Man of the Cloth	www.manofcloth.blogspot.com	designers, inspiration	ZA
Mens Rag	www.mensrag.com	designers	USA
Menswear	www.itsmenswear.wordpress.com	designers, shopping	UK
Mode Parade	www.barimavox.blogspot.com	outfits, diary	UK
My MANy Bags	www.mymanybags.blogspot.com	diary, accessories	SG
Permanent Style	www.permanentstyle.blogspot.com	history	UK
Selectism	www.selectism.com	designers	USA
Street Etiquette	www.streetetiquette.com	outfits, shopping	USA
Style Salvage	www.stylesalvage.blogspot.com	designers, shopping	UK
Suck My Savvy	www.suckmysavvy.blogspot.com	diary, pop culture	USA
Tailored Society	www.tailoredsociety.com	design, designers	USA
The Cablog	www.thecablog.com	dairy, outfits	NOR
The Dandy Project	www.thedandyproject.com	diary, DIY	PHL
The Fashionisto	www.thefashionisto.com	designers	USA
The Life and Times of a Problem Child	www.giancinephile.numeriblog.fr	designers, outfits	F
The Material Boy	www.marcovanrijt.blogspot.com	photography, catwalk, street style	NL
The Sophisticat	www.thesophisticat.blogspot.com	outfits, diary	AUS
The Sunday Best	www.thesundaybest.org	outfits, diary	CAN
The Trad	www.thetrad.blogspot.com	inspiration, lifestyle	USA
Tokyo Dandy	www.tokyodandy.com	pop culture, street style	JP
Un Nouveau Ideal	www.unnouveauideal.typepad.com	diary, designers	GR
Unabashedly Prep	www.unabashedlyprep.com	street style, history	USA
Vogue Adventure	www.vogueadventure.com	models, diary	USA
We Could Grow Up Together	www.wecouldgrowuptogether.blogspot.com	diary, inspiration	CN/USA
What is James Wearing?	www.whatisjameswearing.com	diary, outfits, design	USA

... & BEYOND

BLOG TITLE	URL	TAGS	COUNTRY
Beauty is a Thing of the Past	www.beautyisathingofthepast.blogspot.com	beauty, vintage	USA
Bobby Pin Blog	www.bobbypinblog.blogspot.com	vintage, beauty	USA
CHICtopia	www.chictopia.com	communities, outfits	USA
COACD	www.coacdinc.com	models, photography	USA
Counterfeit Chic	www.counterfeitchic.com	designers, shopping, law	USA
Decade Diary	www.decadediary.typepad.com	illustration, inspiration	USA
Ecouterre	www.ecouterre.com	eco, shopping, lifestyle	USA
Fashion Roundup	www.observer.com/term/fashion-roundup	newspapers, designers, celebrities	USA
Go Fug Yourself	www.gofugyourself.celebuzz.com	celebrities, trends	USA
Heard on the Runway	blogs.wsj.com/runway	newspapers, designers, trends	USA
Hedi Slimane	www.hedislimane.com/diary/index.php	photography	F
I like my style	www.ilikemystyle.net	communities	DE
JUSTJR	blog.justjr.com	collage, designers, runway	F/USA
Karl Lagerfeld's Guide to Life	www.fakekarl.blogspot.com	diary, news, designers	UK
Le Smoking	www.lesmokingimage.blogspot.com	photography, inspiration	USA
Look At Me	www.lookatme.ru/look	street style, communities	RUS
Lookbook	www.lookbook.nu	street style, outfits, communities	USA
Luxiraire	www.luxirare.com	food, photography	USA
Mister Montage	www.mistermontage.com	menswear, collage, pop culture	USA
News from Fashion	www.newsfromfashion.com	illustration	F
On the Runway	runway.blogs.nytimes.com	newspapers, designers, trends	USA
Shoewawa	www.shoewawa.com	accessories, shopping	UK
Sonny photos	www.sonnyphotos.typepad.com	photography, diary	NL
Style like u	www.stylelikeu.com	outfits, inspiration	USA
Talking Fashion	www.teenvogue.com/style/blogs/fashion	magazines, designers, celebrities	USA
The Cut	www.nymag.com/daily/fashion	magazines, designers, celebrities	USA
The Discerning Brute	www.thediscerningbrute.com	eco, menswear, food	USA
The Fader	www.thefader.com/category/style	magazines, designers, shopping	USA
The GQ Eye	www.gq.com/style/blogs/the-gq-eye	magazines, menswear, shopping	USA
The Jason Wu Blog	www.thewstudio.com/blog	designers, news, diary	USA
The Moment	themoment.blogs.nytimes.com	newspapers, design, trends	USA
The Pipeline	www.pipeline.refinery29.com	runway, designers, trends	USA
The Pop	www.thepop.com	magazines, art, designers	UK
The Purse Blog	www.purseblog.com	accessories, shopping	USA
The Unknown Hipster	www.unknownhipster.com	illustration	USA
The Vintage Aficionado	www.defunkd.com/blog	vintage, pop culture	CAN
The Vogue Blog	www.vogue.co.uk/blogs/the-vogue-blog	magazines, designers, lifestyle	UK
Threadbanger	www.threadbanger.com/blog	communities, DIY	USA
V Magazine	www.vmagazine.com/blog.php	magazines, designers	USA
Well Shod, Well Imformed	www.imelda.com.au	accessories, shopping, designers	AUS

BLOG GRAVEYARD

BLOG TITLE	URL	TAGS	COUNTRY
Annie et Carlotta	www.carlottannie.blogspot.com	photography, inspiration, web shop	AUS
Auntie Tati	www.auntietati.blogspot.com	outfits, shopping, vintage	FIN
BrgnStil	www.brgnstil.blogspot.com	street style	NOR
Buenos Aires Street Style	www.ba-street-style.blogspot.com	street style	ARG
Chartreuse Chic	www.chartreusechic.blogspot.com	eco, shopping,	USA
Com On People	www.com-onpeople.blogspot.com	street style, night life	GR
Cuteness burger	www.cutenessburger.com	street style	USA
Dandyism	www.dandyism.net	menswear, history	USA
Diamond Crowns	www.diamondcrowns.blogspot.com	runway, outfits, shopping	CAN
dirtydirtydancing	www.dirtydirtydancing.com	night life	UK
Fashion Orgasm	www.fashionorgasm.blogspot.com	inspiration, celebrities, shopping	USA
Gothic Preppy	www.gothicpreppy.blogspot.com	pop culture, shopping, outfits	USA
I got it at Versayce!	www.igotitatversayce.blogspot.com	designers, shopping, trends	UK
I was there	www.iwas-there.com	night life	USA
It's Her Factory	www.itslasfactory.blogspot.com	outfits, diary	USA
Jottings of a Fashionista	www.jottingsofafashionista.blogspot.com	designers, inspiration, diary	UK
Kicking and Screaming	www.klickingandscreaming.com	night life	USA
Laperolog	www.laperolog.com	night life	F
Mode et Utopie	www.modeutopie.blogspot.com	designers, news, runway	USA
Mode monitor	www.modemonitor.com	shopping, trends, runway	USA
Mr. Peacock	www.mrpeacockstyle.blogspot.com	menswear, shopping, diary	USA
Oslostil	www.oslostil.com	street style	NOR
Pike/pine	www.pikepine.com	street style	USA
Power rangers go	www.powerrangersgo.blogspot.com	designers, inspiration, diary	BE
Reykjavik Looks	www.reykjaviklooks.blogspot.com	street style	IS
Roybotic steez	www.royboticsteez.blogspot.com	runway, designers	CAN
Shiver Me Fantasy	www.afantasizerworld.blogspot.com	diary, outfits, shopping	NL
Strike.Match	www.strike-match.blogspot.com	outfits, inspiration	AUS
Style Bytes	www.stylebytes.net	diary, designers, shopping	NOR
Thecitythecitythecity	www.thecitythecity.wordpress.com	night life	DE
Vegan Vintage	www.veganandvintage.blogspot.com	diary, outfits, vintage	AUS
VIP Girl Style	www.vipgirlstyle.wordpress.com	news, designers, runway	AUS
Young Damsel	www.youngdamsel.blogspot.com	diary, outfits, pop culture	USA

© 2010 Concept & Idea by Kirstin Hanssen
and Felicia Nitzsche
© 2010 the authors
© 2010 Publisher d'jonge Hond
PO Box 1353
8001 BJ Zwolle
The Netherlands
info@dejongehond.nl
www.dejongehond.nl

ISBN 978-90-89-101-52-5 / NUR 452

Publisher: d'jonge Hond
Editors: Kirstin Hanssen (www.kirstinhanssen.nl)
& Elina Tozzi (www.elinatozzi.nl)
Art direction & Design: Felicia Nitzsche
(www.felicianitzsche.com)
Translations: Elina Tozzi
Still Life Photography: Krista van der Niet
(www.kristavanderniet.nl)
Introductions: Marten Mantel, Marieke Ordelmans,
Aynouk Tan, Mrs. Mo Veld, Carlo Wijnands
Photography and Illustrations: kindly supplied
by the bloggers, they hold the copyright unless
otherwise indicated.

We would like to thank:
Micha Bakker, Cheryl Gallaway, Vanessa van
Houtum (Premsela, Dutch Platform for Design
and Fashion), Jeroen Koning, David Stotijn,
and the many bloggers who made this
publication possible.